The Dynasts by Thomas Hardy

AN EPIC-DRAMA OF THE WAR WITH NAPOLEON, IN THREE PARTS.

PART FIRST

The Time covered by the Action being about ten Years

"And I heard sounds of insult, shame, and wrong,
And trumpets blown for wars."

Many giants of Literature originate from the shores of these emerald isles; Shakespeare, Dickens, Chaucer, The Brontes and Austen to which most people would willingly add the name Thomas Hardy.

'Far From The Madding Crowd',' Tess Of The D'Urbervilles', 'The Mayor Of Casterbridge' are but three of his literary masterpieces.

In fact, Hardy himself thought he was a poet who wrote novels purely for the money. Indeed his poems were not published until he was in his fifties after his major novels were published and his reputation set. His novels of course continue to influence and mentor our thoughts.

Each is a journey through a mind that creates characters, landscapes and narratives that reveal themselves in rich and textured detail as few other writers are able to do.

Index of Contents

PREFACE

The Spectacle here presented in the likeness of a Drama is concerned with the Great Historical Calamity, or Clash of Peoples, artificially brought about some hundred years ago.

The choice of such a subject was mainly due to three accidents of locality. It chanced that the writer was familiar with a part of England that lay within hail of the watering-place in which King George the Third had his favourite summer residence during the war with the first Napoleon, and where he was visited by ministers and others who bore the weight of English affairs on their more or less competent shoulders at that stressful time. Secondly, this district, being also near the coast which had echoed with rumours of invasion in their intensest form while the descent threatened, was formerly animated by memories and traditions of the desperate military preparations for that contingency. Thirdly, the same countryside happened to include the village which was the birthplace of Nelson's flag-captain at Trafalgar.

When, as the first published result of these accidents, The Trumpet Major was printed, more than twenty years ago, I found myself in the tantalizing position of having touched the fringe of a vast international tragedy without being able, through limits of plan, knowledge, and opportunity, to enter further into its events; a restriction that prevailed for many years. But the slight regard paid to English influence and action throughout the struggle by those Continental writers who had dealt imaginatively with Napoleon's career, seemed always to leave room for a new handling of the theme which should re-embody the features of this influence in their true proportion; and accordingly, on a belated day about six years back, the following drama was outlined, to be taken up now and then at wide intervals ever since.

It may, I think, claim at least a tolerable fidelity to the facts of its date as they are give in ordinary records. Whenever any evidence of the words really spoken or written by the characters in their various situations was attainable, as close a paraphrase has been aimed at as was compatible with the form chosen. And in all cases outside the oral tradition, accessible scenery, and existing relics, my indebtedness for detail to the abundant pages of the historian, the biographer, and the journalist, English and Foreign, has been, of course, continuous.

It was thought proper to introduce, as supernatural spectators of the terrestrial action, certain impersonated abstractions, or Intelligences, called Spirits. They are intended to be taken by the reader for what they may be worth as contrivances of the fancy merely. Their doctrines are but tentative, and are advanced with little eye to a systematized philosophy warranted to lift "the burthen of the mystery" of this unintelligible world. The chief thing hoped for them is that they and their utterances may have dramatic plausibility enough to procure for them, in the words of Coleridge, "that willing suspension of disbelief for the moment which constitutes poetic faith." The wide prevalence of the Monistic theory of the Universe forbade, in this twentieth century, the importation of Divine personages from any antique Mythology as ready-made sources or channels of Causation, even in verse, and excluded the celestial machinery of, say, Paradise Lost, as peremptorily as that of the Iliad or the Eddas. And the abandonment of the masculine pronoun in allusions to the First or Fundamental Energy seemed a necessary and logical consequence of the long abandonment by thinkers of the anthropomorphic conception of the same. These phantasmal Intelligences are divided into groups, of which one only, that of the Pities, approximates to "the Universal Sympathy of human nature—the spectator idealized" (1) of the Greek Chorus; it is impressionable and inconsistent in its views, which sway hither and thither as wrought on by events. Another group approximates to the passionless Insight of the Ages. The remainder are eclectically chosen auxiliaries whose signification may be readily discerned. In point of literary form, the scheme of contrasted Choruses and other conventions of this external feature was shaped with a single view to the modern expression of a modern outlook, and in frank divergence from classical and other dramatic precedent which ruled the ancient voicings of ancient themes.

It may hardly be necessary to inform readers that in devising this chronicle-piece no attempt has been made to create that completely organic structure of action, and closely-webbed development of character and motive, which are demanded in a drama strictly self- contained. A panoramic show like the present is a series of historical "ordinates" [to use a term in geometry]: the subject is familiar to all; and foreknowledge is assumed to fill in the junctions required to combine the scenes into an artistic unity. Should the mental spectator be unwilling or unable to do this, a historical presentment on an intermittent plan, in which the dramatis personae number some hundreds, exclusive of crowds and armies, becomes in his individual case unsuitable.

In this assumption of a completion of the action by those to whom the drama is addressed, it is interesting, if unnecessary, to name an exemplar as old as Aeschylus, whose plays are, as Dr. Verrall reminds us, (2) scenes from stories taken as known, and would be unintelligible without supplementary scenes of the imagination.

Readers will readily discern, too, that The Dynasts is intended simply for mental performance, and not for the stage. Some critics have averred that to declare a drama (3) as being not for the stage is to make an announcement whose subject and predicate cancel each other. The question seems to be an unimportant matter of terminology. Compositions cast in this shape were, without doubt, originally written for the stage only, and as a consequence their nomenclature of "Act," "Scene," and the like, was drawn directly from the vehicle of representation. But in the course of time such a shape would reveal itself to be an eminently readable one; moreover, by dispensing with the theatre altogether, a freedom of treatment was attainable in this form that was denied where the material possibilities of stagery had to be rigorously remembered. With the careless mechanicism of human speech, the technicalities of practical mumming were retained in these productions when they had ceased to be concerned with the stage at all.

To say, then, in the present case, that a writing in play-shape is not to be played, is merely another way of stating that such writing has been done in a form for which there chances to be no brief definition save one already in use for works that it superficially but not entirely resembles.
Whether mental performance alone may not eventually be the fate of all drama other than that of contemporary or frivolous life, is a kindred question not without interest. The mind naturally flies to the triumphs of the Hellenic and Elizabethan theatre in exhibiting scenes laid "far in the Unapparent," and asks why they should not be repeated. But the meditative world is older, more invidious, more nervous, more quizzical, than it once was, and being unhappily perplexed by—

Riddles of Death Thebes never knew,

may be less ready and less able than Hellas and old England were to look through the insistent, and often grotesque, substance at the thing signified.

In respect of such plays of poesy and dream a practicable compromise may conceivably result, taking the shape of a monotonic delivery of speeches, with dreamy conventional gestures, something in the manner traditionally maintained by the old Christmas mummers, the curiously hypnotizing impressiveness of whose automatic style—that of persons who spoke by no will of their own—may be remembered by all who ever experienced it. Gauzes or screens to blur outlines might still further shut off the actual, as has, indeed, already been done in exceptional cases. But with this branch of the subject we are not concerned here.

T.H.
September 1903.

PART FIRST

CHARACTERS
I. PHANTOM INTELLIGENCES

THE ANCIENT SPIRIT OF THE YEARS/CHORUS OF THE YEARS.
THE SPIRIT OF THE PITIES/CHORUS OF THE PITIES.
SPIRITS SINISTER AND IRONIC/CHORUSES OF SINISTER AND IRONIC SPIRITS.
THE SPIRIT OF RUMOUR/CHORUS OF RUMOURS.
THE SHADE OF THE EARTH.
SPIRIT-MESSENGERS.
RECORDING ANGELS.

II. PERSONS [The names in lower case are mute figures.]
MEN
GEORGE THE THIRD.
The Duke of Cumberland
PITT.
FOX.
SHERIDAN.
WINDHAM.
WHITBREAD.
TIERNEY.
BATHURST AND FULLER.
Lord Chancellor Eldon.
EARL OF MALMESBURY.
LORD MULGRAVE.
ANOTHER CABINET MINISTER.
Lord Grenville.
Viscount Castlereagh.
Viscount Sidmouth.
ANOTHER NOBLE LORD.
ROSE.
Canning.
Perceval.
Grey.
Speaker Abbot.
TOMLINE, BISHOP OF LINCOLN.
SIR WALTER FARQUHAR.
Count Munster.
Other Peers, Ministers, ex-Ministers, Members of Parliament, and Persons of Quality.
....
NELSON.
COLLINGWOOD.
HARDY.
SECRETARY SCOTT.
DR. BEATTY.
DR. MAGRATH.
DR. ALEXANDER SCOTT.
BURKE, PURSER.
Lieutenant Pasco.
ANOTHER LIEUTENANT.
POLLARD, A MIDSHIPMAN.

Captain Adair.
Lieutenants Ram and Whipple.
Other English Naval Officers.
Sergeant-Major Secker and Marines.
Staff and other Officers of the English Army.
A COMPANY OF SOLDIERS.
Regiments of the English Army and Hanoverian.
SAILORS AND BOATMEN.
A MILITIAMAN.
Naval Crews.
....
The Lord Mayor and Corporation of London.
A GENTLEMAN OF FASHION.
WILTSHIRE, A COUNTRY GENTLEMAN
A HORSEMAN.
TWO BEACON-WATCHERS.
ENGLISH CITIZENS AND BURGESSES.
COACH AND OTHER HIGHWAY PASSENGERS.
MESSENGERS, SERVANTS, AND RUSTICS.
....
NAPOLEON BONAPARTE.
DARU, NAPOLEON'S WAR SECRETARY.
LAURISTON, AIDE-DE-CAMP.
MONGE, A PHILOSOPHER.
BERTHIER.
MURAT, BROTHER-IN-LAW OF NAPOLEON.
SOULT.
NEY.
LANNES.
Bernadotte.
Marmont.
Dupont.
Oudinot.
Davout.
Vandamme.
Other French Marshals.
A SUB-OFFICER.
....
VILLENEUVE, NAPOLEON'S ADMIRAL.
DECRES, MINISTER OF MARINE.
FLAG-CAPTAIN MAGENDIE.
LIEUTENANT DAUDIGNON.
LIEUTENANT FOURNIER.
Captain Lucas.
OTHER FRENCH NAVAL OFFICERS AND PETTY OFFICERS.
Seamen of the French and Spanish Navies.
Regiments of the French Army.
COURIERS.

HERALDS.
Aides, Officials, Pages, etc.
ATTENDANTS.
French Citizens.
....
CARDINAL CAPRARA.
Priests, Acolytes, and Choristers.
Italian Doctors and Presidents of Institutions.
Milanese Citizens.
....
THE EMPEROR FRANCIS.
THE ARCHDUKE FERDINAND.
Prince John of Lichtenstien.
PRINCE SCHWARZENBERG.
MACK, AUSTRIAN GENERAL.
JELLACHICH.
RIESC.
WEIROTHER.
ANOTHER AUSTRIAN GENERAL.
TWO AUSTRIAN OFFICERS.
....
The Emperor Alexander.
PRINCE KUTUZOF, RUSSIAN FIELD-MARSHAL.
COUNT LANGERON.
COUNT BUXHOVDEN.
COUNT MILORADOVICH.
DOKHTOROF.
....
Giulay, Gottesheim, Klenau, and Prschebiszewsky.
Regiments of the Austrian Army.
Regiments of the Russian Army.

WOMEN
Queen Charlotte.
English Princesses.
Ladies of the English Court.
LADY HESTER STANHOPE.
A LADY.
Lady Caroline Lamb, Mrs. Damer, and other English Ladies.
....
THE EMPRESS JOSEPHINE.
Princesses and Ladies of Josephine's Court.
Seven Milanese Young Ladies.
....
City- and Towns-women.
Country-women.
A MILITIAMAN'S WIFE.
A STREET-WOMAN.

Ship-women.
Servants.

THE OVERWORLD
[Enter the Ancient Spirit and Chorus of the Years, the Spirit and Chorus of the Pities, the Shade of the Earth, the Spirits Sinister and Ironic with their Choruses, Rumours, Spirit-Messengers, and Recording Angels.]

SHADE OF THE EARTH
What of the Immanent Will and Its designs?

SPIRIT OF THE YEARS
It works unconsciously, as heretofore,
Eternal artistries in Circumstance,
Whose patterns, wrought by rapt aesthetic rote,
Seem in themselves Its single listless aim,
And not their consequence.

CHORUS OF THE PITIES [aerial music]
Still thus? Still thus?
Ever unconscious!
An automatic sense
Unweeting why or whence?
Be, then, the inevitable, as of old,
Although that SO it be we dare not hold!

SPIRIT OF THE YEARS
Hold what ye list, fond believing Sprites,
You cannot swerve the pulsion of the Byss,
Which thinking on, yet weighing not Its thought,
Unchecks Its clock-like laws.

SPIRIT SINISTER [aside]
Good, as before.
My little engines, then, will still have play.

SPIRIT OF THE PITIES
Why doth It so and so, and ever so,
This viewless, voiceless Turner of the Wheel?

SPIRIT OF THE YEARS
As one sad story runs, It lends Its heed
To other worlds, being wearied out with this;

Wherefore Its mindlessness of earthly woes.
Some, too, have told at whiles that rightfully
Its warefulness, Its care, this planet lost
When in her early growth and crudity
By bad mad acts of severance men contrived,
Working such nescience by their own device.—
Yea, so it stands in certain chronicles,
Though not in mine.

SPIRIT OF THE PITIES
Meet is it, none the less,
To bear in thought that though Its consciousness
May be estranged, engrossed afar, or sealed,
Sublunar shocks may wake Its watch anon?

SPIRIT OF THE YEARS
Nay. In the Foretime, even to the germ of Being,
Nothing appears of shape to indicate
That cognizance has marshalled things terrene,
Or will [such is my thinking] in my span.
Rather they show that, like a knitter drowsed,
Whose fingers play in skilled unmindfulness,
The Will has woven with an absent heed
Since life first was; and ever will so weave.

SPIRIT SINISTER
Hence we've rare dramas going—more so since
It wove Its web in the Ajaccian womb!

SPIRIT OF THE YEARS
Well, no more this on what no mind can mete.
Our scope is but to register and watch
By means of this great gift accorded us—
The free trajection of our entities.

SPIRIT OF THE PITIES
On things terrene, then, I would say that though
The human news wherewith the Rumours stirred us
May please thy temper, Years, 'twere better far
Such deeds were nulled, and this strange man's career
Wound up, as making inharmonious jars
In her creation whose meek wraith we know.
The more that he, turned man of mere traditions,
Now profits naught. For the large potencies
Instilled into his idiosyncrasy—
To throne fair Liberty in Privilege' room—
Are taking taint, and sink to common plots
For his own gain.

SHADE OF THE EARTH
And who, then, Cordial One,
Wouldst substitute for this Intractable?

CHORUS OF THE EARTH
We would establish those of kindlier build,
In fair Compassions skilled,
Men of deep art in life-development;
Watchers and warders of thy varied lands,
Men surfeited of laying heavy hands,
Upon the innocent,
The mild, the fragile, the obscure content
Among the myriads of thy family.
Those, too, who love the true, the excellent,
And make their daily moves a melody.

SHADE OF THE EARTH
They may come, will they. I am not averse.
Yet know I am but the ineffectual Shade
Of her the Travailler, herself a thrall
To It; in all her labourings curbed and kinged!

SPIRIT OF THE YEARS
Shall such be mooted now? Already change
Hath played strange pranks since first I brooded here.
But old Laws operate yet; and phase and phase
Of men's dynastic and imperial moils
Shape on accustomed lines. Though, as for me,
I care not thy shape, or what they be.

SPIRIT OF THE PITIES
You seem to have small sense of mercy, Sire?

SPIRIT OF THE YEARS
Mercy I view, not urge;—nor more than mark
What designate your titles Good and Ill.
'Tis not in me to feel with, or against,
These flesh-hinged mannikins Its hand upwinds
To click-clack off Its preadjusted laws;
But only through my centuries to behold
Their aspects, and their movements, and their mould.

SPIRIT OF THE PITIES
They are shapes that bleed, mere mannikins or no,
And each has parcel in the total Will.

SPIRIT OF THE YEARS

Which overrides them as a whole its parts
In other entities.

SPIRIT SINISTER [aside]
Limbs of Itself:
Each one a jot of It in quaint disguise?
I'll fear all men henceforward!

SPIRIT OF THE PITIES
Go to. Let this terrestrial tragedy—

SPIRIT IRONIC
Nay, Comedy—

SPIRIT OF THE PITIES
Let this earth-tragedy
Whereof we spake, afford a spectacle
Forthwith conned closelier than your custom is.—

SPIRIT OF THE YEARS
How does it stand? [To a Recording Angel]
Open and chant the page
Thou'st lately writ, that sums these happenings,
In brief reminder of their instant points
Slighted by us amid our converse here.

RECORDING ANGEL [from a book, in recitative]
Now mellow-eyed Peace is made captive,
And Vengeance is chartered
To deal forth its dooms on the Peoples
With sword and with spear.

Men's musings are busy with forecasts
Of muster and battle,
And visions of shock and disaster
Rise red on the year.

The easternmost ruler sits wistful,
And tense he to midward;
The King to the west mans his borders
In front and in rear.

While one they eye, flushed from his crowning,
Ranks legions around him
To shake the enisled neighbour nation
And close her career!

SEMICHORUS I OF RUMOURS [aerial music]

O woven-winged squadrons of Toulon
And fellows of Rochefort,
Wait, wait for a wind, and draw westward
Ere Nelson be near!

For he reads not your force, or your freightage
Of warriors fell-handed,
Or when they will join for the onset,
Or whither they steer!

SEMICHORUS II
O Nelson, so zealous a watcher
Through months-long of cruizing,
Thy foes may elide thee a moment,
Put forth, and get clear;

And rendezvous westerly straightway
With Spain's aiding navies,
And hasten to head violation
Of Albion's frontier!

SPIRIT OF THE YEARS
Methinks too much assurance thrills your note
On secrets in my locker, gentle sprites;
But it may serve.—Our thought being now reflexed
To forces operant on this English isle,
Behoves it us to enter scene by scene,
And watch the spectacle of Europe's moves
In her embroil, as they were self-ordained
According to the naive and liberal creed
Of our great-hearted young Compassionates,
Forgetting the Prime Mover of the gear,
As puppet-watchers him who pulls the strings.—
You'll mark the twitchings of this Bonaparte
As he with other figures foots his reel,
Until he twitch him into his lonely grave:
Also regard the frail ones that his flings
Have made gyrate like animalcula
In tepid pools.—Hence to the precinct, then,
And count as framework to the stagery
Yon architraves of sunbeam-smitten cloud.—
So may ye judge Earth's jackaclocks to be
No fugled by one Will, but function-free.

[The nether sky opens, and Europe is disclosed as a prone and emaciated figure, the Alps shaping like a
backbone, and the branching mountain-chains like ribs, the peninsular plateau of Spain forming a head.
Broad and lengthy lowlands stretch from the north of France across Russia like a grey-green garment
hemmed by the Ural mountains and the glistening Arctic Ocean.

The point of view then sinks downwards through space, and draws near to the surface of the perturbed countries, where the peoples, distressed by events which they did not cause, are seen writhing, crawling, heaving, and vibrating in their various cities and nationalities.]

SPIRIT OF THE YEARS [to the Spirit of the Pities]
As key-scene to the whole, I first lay bare
The Will-webs of thy fearful questioning;
For know that of my antique privileges
This gift to visualize the Mode is one
[Though by exhaustive strain and effort only].
See, then, and learn, ere my power pass again.

[A new and penetrating light descends on the spectacle, enduring men and things with a seeming transparency, and exhibiting as one organism the anatomy of life and movement in all humanity and vitalized matter included in the display.]

SPIRIT OF THE PITIES
Amid this scene of bodies substantive
Strange waves I sight like winds grown visible,
Which bear men's forms on their innumerous coils,
Twining and serpenting round and through.
Also retracting threads like gossamers—
Except in being irresistible—
Which complicate with some, and balance all.

SPIRIT OF THE YEARS
These are the Prime Volitions,—fibrils, veins,
Will-tissues, nerves, and pulses of the Cause,
That heave throughout the Earth's compositure.
Their sum is like the lobule of a Brain
Evolving always that it wots not of;
A Brain whose whole connotes the Everywhere,
And whose procedure may but be discerned
By phantom eyes like ours; the while unguessed
Of those it stirs, who [even as ye do] dream
Their motions free, their orderings supreme;
Each life apart from each, with power to mete
Its own day's measures; balanced, self complete;
Though they subsist but atoms of the One
Labouring through all, divisible from none;
But this no further now. Deem yet man's deeds self-done.

GENERAL CHORUS OF INTELLIGENCES [aerial music]
We'll close up Time, as a bird its van,
We'll traverse Space, as spirits can,
Link pulses severed by leagues and years,
Bring cradles into touch with biers;

So that the far-off Consequence appear
Prompt at the heel of foregone Cause.—
The PRIME, that willed ere wareness was,
Whose Brain perchance is Space, whose Thought its laws,
Which we as threads and streams discern,
We may but muse on, never learn.

END OF THE FORE SCENE

ACT FIRST

SCENE I

ENGLAND. A RIDGE IN WESSEX

[The time is a fine day in March 1805. A highway crosses the ridge, which is near the sea, and the south coast is seen bounding the landscape below, the open Channel extending beyond.]

SPIRITS OF THE YEARS
Hark now, and gather how the martial mood
Stirs England's humblest hearts. Anon we'll trace
Its heavings in the upper coteries there.

SPIRIT SINISTER
Ay; begin small, and so lead up to the greater. It is a sound dramatic principle. I always aim to follow it in my pestilences, fires, famines, and other comedies. And though, to be sure, I did not in my Lisbon earthquake, I did in my French Terror, and my St. Domingo burlesque.

SPIRIT OF THE YEARS
Thy Lisbon earthquake, Thy French Terror. Wait.
Thinking thou will'st, thou dost but indicate.

[A stage-coach enters, with passengers outside. Their voices after the foregoing sound small and commonplace, as from another medium.]

FIRST PASSENGER
There seems to be a deal of traffic over Ridgeway, even at this time o' year.

SECOND PASSENGER
Yes. It is because the King and Court are coming down here later on. They wake up this part rarely!... See, now, how the Channel and coast open out like a chart. That patch of mist below us is the town we are bound for. There's the Isle of Slingers beyond, like a floating snail. That wide bay on the right is where the "Abergavenny," Captain John Wordsworth, was wrecked last month. One can see half across to France up here.

FIRST PASSENGER

Half across. And then another little half, and then all that's behind—the Corsican mischief!

SECOND PASSENGER
Yes. People who live hereabout—I am a native of these parts—feel the nearness of France more than they do inland.

FIRST PASSENGER
That's why we have seen so many of these marching regiments on the road. This year his grandest attempt upon us is to be made, I reckon.

SECOND PASSENGER
May we be ready!

FIRST PASSENGER
Well, we ought to be. We've had alarms enough, God knows.

[Some companies of infantry are seen ahead, and the coach presently overtakes them.]

SOLDIERS [singing as they walk]
We be the King's men, hale and hearty,
Marching to meet one Buonaparty;
If he won't sail, lest the wind should blow,
We shall have marched for nothing, O!
Right fol-lol!

We be the King's men, hale and hearty,
Marching to meet one Buonaparty;
If he be sea-sick, says "No, no!"
We shall have marched for nothing, O!
Right fol-lol!

[The soldiers draw aside, and the coach passes on.]

SECOND PASSENGER
Is there truth in it that Bonaparte wrote a letter to the King last month?

FIRST PASSENGER
Yes, sir. A letter in his own hand, in which he expected the King to reply to him in the same manner.

SOLDIERS [continuing, as they are left behind]
We be the King's men, hale and hearty,
Marching to meet one Buonaparty;
Never mind, mates; we'll be merry, though
We may have marched for nothing, O!
Right fol-lol!

THIRD PASSENGER
And was Boney's letter friendly?

FIRST PASSENGER
Certainly, sir. He requested peace with the King.

THIRD PASSENGER
And why shouldn't the King reply in the same manner?

FIRST PASSENGER
What! Encourage this man in an act of shameless presumption, and give him the pleasure of considering himself the equal of the King of England—whom he actually calls his brother!

THIRD PASSENGER
He must be taken for what he is, not for what he was; and if he calls King George his brother it doesn't speak badly for his friendliness.

FIRST PASSENGER
Whether or no, the King, rightly enough, did not reply in person, but through Lord Mulgrave our Foreign Minister, to the effect that his Britannic Majesty cannot give a specific answer till he has communicated with the Continental powers.

THIRD PASSENGER
Both the manner and the matter of the reply are British; but a huge mistake.

FIRST PASSENGER
Sir, am I to deem you a friend of Bonaparte, a traitor to your country—

THIRD PASSENGER
Damn my wig, sir, if I'll be called a traitor by you or any Court sycophant at all at all!

[He unpacks a case of pistols.]

SECOND PASSENGER
Gentlemen forbear, forbear! Should such differences be suffered to arise on a spot where we may, in less than three months, be fighting for our very existence? This is foolish, I say. Heaven alone, who reads the secrets of this man's heart, can tell what his meaning and intent may be, and if his letter has been answered wisely or no.

[The coach is stopped to skid the wheel for the descent of the hill, and before it starts again a dusty horseman overtakes it.]

SEVERAL PASSENGERS
A London messenger! [To horseman] Any news, sir? We are from Bristol only.

HORSEMAN
Yes; much. We have declared war against Spain, an error giving vast delight to France. Bonaparte says he will date his next dispatches from London, and the landing of his army may be daily expected.

[Exit horseman.]

THIRD PASSENGER
Sir, I apologize. He's not to be trusted! War is his name, and aggression is with him!

[He repacks the pistols. A silence follows. The coach and passengers move downwards and disappear towards the coast.]

SPIRIT OF THE PITIES
Ill chanced it that the English monarch George
Did not respond to the said Emperor!

SPIRIT SINISTER
I saw good sport therein, and paean'd the Will
To unimpel so stultifying a move!
Which would have marred the European broil,
And sheathed all swords, and silenced every gun
That riddles human flesh.

SPIRIT OF THE PITIES
O say no more;
If aught could gratify the Absolute
'Twould verily be thy censure, not thy praise!

SPIRIT OF THE YEARS
The ruling was that we should witness things
And not dispute them. To the drama, then.
Emprizes over-Channel are the key
To this land's stir and ferment.—Thither we.

[Clouds gather over the scene, and slowly open elsewhere.]

SCENE II

PARIS. OFFICE OF THE MINISTER OF MARINE

[ADMIRAL DECRES seated at a table. A knock without.]

DECRES
Come in! Good news, I hope!

[An attendant enters.]

ATTENDANT
A courier, sir.

DECRES

Show him in straightway.

[The attendant goes out.]

From the Emperor
As I expected!

COURIER
Sir, for your own hand
And yours alone.

DECRES
Thanks. Be in waiting near.

[The courier withdraws.]

DECRES reads:
"I am resolved that no wild dream of Ind,
And what we there might win; or of the West,
And bold re-conquest there of Surinam
And other Dutch retreats along those coasts,
Or British islands nigh, shall draw me now
From piercing into England through Boulogne
As lined in my first plan. If I do strike,
I strike effectively; to forge which feat
There's but one way—planting a mortal wound
In England's heart—the very English land—
Whose insolent and cynical reply
To my well-based complaint on breach of faith
Concerning Malta, as at Amiens pledged,
Has lighted up anew such flames of ire
As may involve the world.—Now to the case:
Our naval forces can be all assembled
Without the foe's foreknowledge or surmise,
By these rules following; to whose text I ask
Your gravest application; and, when conned,
That steadfastly you stand by word and word,
Making no question of one jot therein.

"First, then, let Villeneuve wait a favouring wind
For process westward swift to Martinique,
Coaxing the English after. Join him there
Gravina, Missiessy, and Ganteaume;
Which junction once effected all our keels—
While the pursuers linger in the West
At hopeless fault.—Having hoodwinked them thus,
Our boats skim over, disembark the army,
And in the twinkling of a patriot's eye

All London will be ours.

"In strictest secrecy carve this to shape—
Let never an admiral or captain scent
Save Villeneuve and Ganteaume; and pen each charge
With your own quill. The surelier to outwit them
I start for Italy; and there, as 'twere
Engrossed in fetes and Coronation rites,
Abide till, at the need, I reach Boulogne,
And head the enterprize.—NAPOLEON."

[DECRES reflects, and turns to write.]

SPIRIT OF THE YEARS
He buckles to the work. First to Villeneuve,
His onetime companion and his boyhood's friend,
Now lingering at Toulon, he jots swift lines,
The duly to Ganteaume.—They are sealed forthwith,
And superscribed: "Break not till on the main."

[Boisterous singing is heard in the street.]

SPIRIT OF THE PITIES
I hear confused and simmering sounds without,
Like those which thrill the hives at evenfall
When swarming pends.

SPIRIT OF THE YEARS
They but proclaim the crowd,
Which sings and shouts its hot enthusiasms
For this dead-ripe design on England's shore,
Till the persuasion of its own plump words,
Acting upon mercurial temperaments,
Makes hope as prophecy. "Our Emperor
Will show himself [say they] in this exploit
Unwavering, keen, and irresistible
As is the lightning prong. Our vast flotillas
Have been embodied as by sorcery;
Soldiers made seamen, and the ports transformed
To rocking cities casemented with guns.
Against these valiants balance England's means:
Raw merchant-fellows from the counting-house,
Raw labourers from the fields, who thumb for arms
Clumsy untempered pikes forged hurriedly,
And cry them full-equipt. Their batteries,
Their flying carriages, their catamarans,
Shall profit not, and in one summer night
We'll find us there!"

RECORDING ANGEL
And is this prophecy true?

SPIRIT OF THE YEARS
Occasion will reveal.

SHADE OF EARTH
What boots it, Sire,
To down this dynasty, set that one up,
Goad panting peoples to the throes thereof,
Make wither here my fruit, maintain it there,
And hold me travailling through fineless years
In vain and objectless monotony,
When all such tedious conjuring could be shunned
By uncreation? Howsoever wise
The governance of these massed mortalities,
A juster wisdom his who should have ruled
They had not been.

SPIRIT OF THE YEARS
Nay, something hidden urged
The giving matter motion; and these coils
Are, maybe, good as any.

SPIRIT OF THE PITIES
But why any?

SPIRIT OF THE YEARS
Sprite of Compassions, ask the Immanent!
I am but an accessory of Its works,
Whom the Ages render conscious; and at most
Figure as bounden witness of Its laws.

SPIRIT OF THE PITIES
How ask the aim of unrelaxing Will?
Tranced in Its purpose to unknowingness?
[If thy words, Ancient Phantom, token true.]

SPIRIT OF THE YEARS
Thou answerest well. But cease to ask of me.
Meanwhile the mime proceeds.—We turn herefrom,
Change our homuncules, and observe forthwith
How the High Influence sways the English realm,
And how the jacks lip out their reasonings there.

[The Cloud-curtain draws.]

SCENE III

LONDON. THE OLD HOUSE OF COMMONS

[A long chamber with a gallery on each side supported by thin columns having gilt Ionic capitals. Three round-headed windows are at the further end, above the Speaker's chair, which is backed by a huge pedimented structure in white and gilt, surmounted by the lion and the unicorn. The windows are uncurtained, one being open, through which some boughs are seen waving in the midnight gloom without. Wax candles, burnt low, wave and gutter in a brass chandelier which hangs from the middle of the ceiling, and in branches projecting from the galleries.

The House is sitting, the benches, which extend round to the Speaker's elbows, being closely packed, and the galleries likewise full. Among the members present on the Government side are PITT and other ministers with their supporters, including CANNING, CASTLEREAGH, LORD C. SOMERSET, ERSKINE, W. DUNDAS, HUSKISSON, ROSE, BEST, ELLIOT, DALLAS, and the general body of the party. On the opposite side are noticeable FOX, SHERIDAN, WINDHAM, WHITBREAD, GREY, T. GRENVILLE, TIERNEY, EARL TEMPLE, PONSONBY, G. AND H. WALPOLE, DUDLEY NORTH, and TIMOTHY SHELLEY. Speaker ABBOT occupies the Chair.]

SPIRIT OF THE YEARS
As prelude to the scene, as means to aid
Our younger comrades in its construing,
Pray spread your scripture, and rehearse in brief
The reasonings here of late—to whose effects
Words of to-night form sequence.

[The Recording Angels chant from their books, antiphonally, in a minor recitative.]

ANGEL I [aerial music]
Feeble-framed dull unresolve, unresourcefulness,
Sat in the halls of the Kingdom's high Councillors,
Whence the grey glooms of a ghost-eyed despondency
Wanned as with winter the national mind.

ANGEL II
England stands forth to the sword of Napoleon
Nakedly—not an ally in support of her;
Men and munitions dispersed inexpediently;
Projects of range and scope poorly defined.

ANGEL I
Once more doth Pitt deem the land crying loud to him.—
Frail though and spent, and an-hungered for restfulness
Once more responds he, dead fervours to energize,
Aims to concentre, slack efforts to bind.

ANGEL II
Ere the first fruit thereof grow audible,
Holding as hapless his dream of good guardianship,
Jestingly, earnestly, shouting it serviceless,
Tardy, inept, and uncouthly designed.

ANGELS I AND II
So now, to-night, in slashing old sentences,
Hear them speak,—gravely these, those with gay-heartedness,—
Midst their admonishments little conceiving how
Scarlet the scroll that the years will unwind!

SPIRIT OF THE PITIES [to the Spirit of the Years]
Let us put on and suffer for the nonce
The feverish fleshings of Humanity,
And join the pale debaters here convened.
So may thy soul be won to sympathy
By donning their poor mould.

SPIRIT OF THE YEARS
I'll humour thee,
Though my unpassioned essence could not change
Did I incarn in moulds of all mankind!

SPIRIT IRONIC
'Tis enough to make every little dog in England run to mixen to hear this Pitt sung so strenuously! I'll be
the third of the incarnate, on the chance of hearing the tune played the other way.

SPIRIT SINISTER
And I the fourth. There's sure to be something in my line toward, where politicians gathered together!

[The four Phantoms enter the Gallery of the House in the disguise of ordinary strangers.]

SHERIDAN [rising]
The Bill I would have leave to introduce
Is framed, sir, to repeal last Session's Act,
By party-scribes intituled a Provision
For England's Proper Guard; but elsewhere known
As Mr. Pitt's new Patent Parish Pill. [Laughter.]

The ministerial countenances, I mark,
Congeal to dazed surprise at my straight motion—
Why, passes sane conjecture. It may be
That, with a haughty and unwavering faith
In their own battering-rams of argument,
They deemed our buoyance whelmed, and sapped, and sunk
To our hope's sheer bottom, whence a miracle
Was all could friend and float us; or, maybe,

They are amazed at our rude disrespect
In making mockery of an English Law
Sprung sacred from the King's own Premier's brain!
—I hear them snort; but let them wince at will,
My duty must be done; shall be done quickly
By citing some few facts.

An Act for our defence!
It weakens, not defends; and oversea
Swoln France's despot and his myrmidons
This moment know it, and can scoff thereat.
Our people know it too—those who can peer
Behind the scenes of this poor painted show
Called soldiering!—The Act has failed, must fail,
As my right honourable friend well proved
When speaking t'other night, whose silencing
By his right honourable vis a vis
Was of the genuine Governmental sort,
And like the catamarans their sapience shaped
All fizzle and no harm. [Laughter.] The Act, in brief,
Effects this much: that the whole force of England
Is strengthened by—eleven thousand men!
So sorted that the British infantry
Are now eight hundred less than heretofore!

In Ireland, where the glamouring influence
Of the right honourable gentleman
Prevails with magic might, ELEVEN men
Have been amassed. And in the Cinque-Port towns,
Where he is held in absolute veneration,
His method has so quickened martial fire
As to bring in—one man. O would that man
Might meet my sight! [Laughter.] A Hercules, no doubt,
A god-like emanation from this Act,
Who with his single arm will overthrow
All Buonaparte's legions ere their keels
Have scraped one pebble of our fortless shore!...
Such is my motion, sir, and such my mind.

[He sits down amid cheers. The candle-snuffers go round, and Pitt rises. During the momentary pause
before he speaks the House assumes an attentive stillness, in which can be heard the rustling of the
trees without, a horn from an early coach, and the voice of the watch crying the hour.]

PITT
Not one on this side but appreciates
Those mental gems and airy pleasantries
Flashed by the honourable gentleman,
Who shines in them by birthright. Each device

Of drollery he has laboured to outshape,
[Or treasured up from others who have shaped it,]
Displays that are the conjurings of the moment,
[Or mellowed and matured by sleeping on]—
Dry hoardings in his book of commonplace,
Stored without stint of toil through days and months—
He heaps into one mass, and light and fans
As fuel for his flaming eloquence,
Mouthed and maintained without a thought or care
If germane to the theme, or not at all.

Now vain indeed it were should I assay
To match him in such sort. For, sir, alas,
To use imagination as the ground
Of chronicle, take myth and merry tale
As texts for prophecy, is not my gift
Being but a person primed with simple fact,
Unprinked by jewelled art.—But to the thing.

The preparations of the enemy,
Doggedly bent to desolate our land,
Advance with a sustained activity.
They are seen, they are known, by you and by us all.
But they evince no clear-eyed tentative
In furtherance of the threat, whose coming off,
Ay, years may yet postpone; whereby the Act
Will far outstrip him, and the thousands called
Duly to join the ranks by its provisions,
In process sure, if slow, will ratch the lines
Of English regiments—seasoned, cool, resolved—
To glorious length and firm prepotency.
And why, then, should we dream of its repeal
Ere profiting by its advantages?
Must the House listen to such wilding words
As this proposal, at the very hour
When the Act's gearing finds its ordered grooves
And circles into full utility?
The motion of the honourable gentleman
Reminds me aptly of a publican
Who should, when malting, mixing, mashing's past,
Fermenting, barrelling, and spigoting,
Quick taste the brew, and shake his sapient head,
And cry in acid voice: The ale is new!
Brew old, you varlets; cast this slop away! [Cheers.]

But gravely, sir, I would conclude to-night,
And, as a serious man on serious things,
I now speak here.... I pledge myself to this:

Unprecedented and magnificent
As were our strivings in the previous war,
Our efforts in the present shall transcend them,
As men will learn. Such efforts are not sized
By this light measuring-rule my critic here
Whips from his pocket like a clerk-o'-works!...
Tasking and toilsome war's details must be,
And toilsome, too, must be their criticism,—
Not in a moment's stroke extemporized.

The strange fatality that haunts the times
Wherein our lot is cast, has no example.
Times are they fraught with peril, trouble, gloom;
We have to mark their lourings, and to face them.
Sir, reading thus the full significance
Of these big days, large though my lackings be,
Can any hold of those who know my past
That I, of all men, slight our safeguarding?
No: by all honour no!—Were I convinced
That such could be the mind of members here,
My sorrowing thereat would doubly shade
The shade on England now! So I do trust
All in the House will take my tendered word,
And credit my deliverance here to-night,
That in this vital point of watch and ward
Against the threatenings from yonder coast
We stand prepared; and under Providence
Shall fend whatever hid or open stroke
A foe may deal.

[He sits down amid loud ministerial cheers, with symptoms of great exhaustion.]

WINDHAM
The question that compels the House to-night
Is not of differences in wit and wit,
But if for England it be well or no
To null the new-fledged Act, as one inept
For setting up with speed and hot effect
The red machinery of desperate war.—
Whatever it may do, or not, it stands,
A statesman' raw experiment. If ill,
Shall more experiments and more be tried
In stress of jeopardy that stirs demand
For sureness of proceeding? Must this House
Exchange safe action based on practised lines
For yet more ventures into risks unknown
To gratify a quaint projector's whim,
While enemies hang grinning round our gates

To profit by mistake?

My friend who spoke
Found comedy in the matter. Comical
As it may be in parentage and feature,
Most grave and tragic in its consequence
This Act may prove. We are moving thoughtlessly,
We squander precious, brief, life-saving time
On idle guess-games. Fail the measure must,
Nay, failed it has already; and should rouse
Resolve in its progenitor himself
To move for its repeal! [Cheers.]

WHITBREAD
I rise but to subjoin a phrase or two
To those of my right honourable friend.
I, too, am one who reads the present pinch
As passing all our risks heretofore.
For why? Our bold and reckless enemy,
Relaxing not his plans, has treasured time
To mass his monstrous force on all the coigns
From which our coast is close assailable.
Ay, even afloat his concentrations work:
Two vast united squadrons of his sail
Move at this moment viewless on the seas.—
Their whereabouts, untraced, unguessable,
Will not be known to us till some black blow
Be dealt by them in some undreamt-of quarter
To knell our rule.

That we are reasonably enfenced therefrom
By such an Act is but a madman's dream....
A commonwealth so situate cries aloud
For more, far mightier, measures! End an Act
In Heaven's name, then, which only can obstruct
The fabrication of more trusty tackle
For building up an army! [Cheers.]

BATHURST
Sir, the point
To any sober mind is bright as noon;
Whether the Act should have befitting trial
Or be blasphemed at sight. I firmly hold
The latter loud iniquity.—One task
Is theirs who would inter this corpse-cold Act—
[So said]—to bring to birth a substitute!
Sir, they have none; they have given no thought to one,
And this their deeds incautiously disclose

Their cloaked intention and most secret aim!
With them the question is not how to frame
A finer trick to trounce intrusive foes,
But who shall be the future ministers
To whom such trick against intrusive foes,
Whatever it may prove, shall be entrusted!
They even ask the country gentlemen
To join them in this job. But, God be praised,
Those gentlemen are sound, and of repute;
Their names, their attainments, and their blood,
[Ironical Opposition cheers.]
Safeguard them from an onslaught on an Act
For ends so sinister and palpable! [Cheers and jeerings.]

FULLER
I disapprove of censures of the Act.—
All who would entertain such hostile thought
Would swear that black is white, that night is day.
No honest man will join a reckless crew
Who'd overthrow their country for their gain! [Laughter.]

TIERNEY
It is incumbent on me to declare
In the last speaker's face my censure, based
On grounds most clear and constitutional.—
An Act it is that studies to create
A standing army, large and permanent;
Which kind of force has ever been beheld
With jealous-eyed disfavour in this House.
It makes for sure oppression, binding men
To serve for less than service proves it worth
Conditioned by no hampering penalty.
For these and late-spoke reasons, then, I say,
Let not the Act deface the statute-book,
But blot it out forthwith. [Hear, hear.]

FOX [rising amid cheers]
At this late hour,
After the riddling fire the Act has drawn on't,
My words shall hold the House the briefest while.
Too obvious to the most unwilling mind
It grows that the existence of this law
Experience and reflection have condemned.
Professing to do much, it makes for nothing;
Not only so; while feeble in effect
It shows it vicious in its principle.
Engaging to raise men for the common weal
It sets a harmful and unequal tax

Capriciously on our communities.—
The annals of a century fail to show
More flagrant cases of oppressiveness
Than those this statute works to perpetrate,
Which [like all Bills this favoured statesman frames,
And clothes with tapestries of rhetoric
Disguising their real web of commonplace]
Though held as shaped for English bulwarking,
Breathes in its heart perversities of party,
And instincts toward oligarchic power,
Galling the many to relieve the few! [Cheers.]

Whatever breadth and sense of equity
Inform the methods of this minister,
Those mitigants nearly always trace their root
To measures that his predecessors wrought.
And ere his Government can dare assert
Superior claim to England's confidence,
They owe it to their honour and good name
To furnish better proof of such a claim
Than is revealed by the abortiveness
Of this thing called an Act for our Defence.

To the great gifts of its artificer
No member of this House is more disposed
To yield full recognition than am I.
No man has found more reason so to do
Through the long roll of disputatious years
Wherein we have stood opposed....
But if one single fact could counsel me
To entertain a doubt of those great gifts,
And cancel faith in his capacity,
That fact would be the vast imprudence shown
In staking recklessly repute like his
On such an Act as he has offered us—
So false in principle, so poor in fruit.
Sir, the achievements and effects thereof
Have furnished not one fragile argument
Which all the partiality of friendship
Can kindle to consider as the mark
Of a clear, vigorous, freedom-fostering mind!

[He sits down amid lengthy cheering from the Opposition.]

SHERIDAN
My summary shall be brief, and to the point.—
The said right honourable Prime Minister
Has thought it proper to declare my speech

The jesting of an irresponsible;—
Words from a person who has never read
The Act he claims him urgent to repeal.
Such quips and qizzings [as he reckons them]
He implicates as gathered from long hoards
Stored up with cruel care, to be discharged
With sudden blaze of pyrotechnic art
On the devoted, gentle, shrinking head
O' the right incomparable gentleman! [Laughter.]
But were my humble, solemn, sad oration [Laughter.]
Indeed such rattle as he rated it,
Is it not strange, and passing precedent,
That the illustrious chief of Government
Should have uprisen with such indecent speed
And strenuously replied? He, sir, knows well
That vast and luminous talents like his own
Could not have been demanded to choke off
A witcraft marked by nothing more of weight
Than ignorant irregularity!
Nec Deus intersit—and so-and-so—
Is a well-worn citation whose close fit
None will perceive more clearly in the Fane
Than its presiding Deity opposite. [Laughter.]
His thunderous answer thus perforce condemns him!

Moreover, to top all, the while replying,
He still thought best to leave intact the reasons
On which my blame was founded!
Thus, them, stands
My motion unimpaired, convicting clearly
Of dire perversion that capacity
We formerly admired.— [Cries of "Oh, oh."]
This minister
Whose circumventions never circumvent,
Whose coalitions fail to coalesce;
This dab at secret treaties known to all,
This darling of the aristocracy—

[Laughter, "Oh, oh," cheers, and cries of "Divide."]

Has brought the millions to the verge of ruin,
By pledging them to Continental quarrels
Of which we see no end! [Cheers.]

[The members rise to divide.]

SPIRIT OF THE PITIES
It irks me that they thus should Yea and Nay

As though a power lay in their oraclings,
If each decision work unconsciously,
And would be operant though unloosened were
A single lip!

SPIRIT OF RUMOUR
There may react on things
Some influence from these, indefinitely,
And even on That, whose outcome we all are.

SPIRIT OF THE YEARS
Hypotheses!—More boots it to remind
The younger here of our ethereal band
And hierarchy of Intelligences,
That this thwart Parliament whose moods we watch—
So insular, empiric, un-ideal—
May figure forth in sharp and salient lines
To retrospective eyes of afterdays,
And print its legend large on History.
For one cause—if I read the signs aright—
To-night's appearance of its Minister
In the assembly of his long-time sway
Is near his last, and themes to-night launched forth
Will take a tincture from that memory,
When me recall the scene and circumstance
That hung about his pleadings.—But no more;
The ritual of each party is rehearsed,
Dislodging not one vote or prejudice;
The ministers their ministries retain,
And Ins as Ins, and Outs as Outs, remain.

SPIRIT OF THE PITIES
Meanwhile what of the Foeman's vast array
That wakes these tones?

SPIRIT OF THE YEARS
Abide the event, young Shade:
Soon stars will shut and show a spring-eyed dawn,
And sunbeams fountain forth, that will arouse
Those forming bands to full activity.

[An honourable member reports that he spies strangers.]

A timely token that we dally here!
We now cast off these mortal manacles,
And speed us seaward.

[The Phantoms vanish from the Gallery. The members file out to the lobbies. The House and Westminster recede into the films of night, and the point of observation shifts rapidly across the Channel.]

THE HARBOUR OF BOULOGNE

[The morning breaks, radiant with early sunlight. The French Army of Invasion is disclosed. On the hills on either side of the town and behind appear large military camps formed of timber huts. Lower down are other camps of more or less permanent kind, the whole affording accommodation for one hundred and fifty thousand men.

South of the town is an extensive basin surrounded by quays, the heaps of fresh soil around showing it to be a recent excavation from the banks of the Liane. The basin is crowded with the flotilla, consisting of hundreds of vessels of sundry kinds: flat-bottomed brigs with guns and two masts; boats of one mast, carrying each an artillery waggon, two guns, and a two-stalled horse-box; transports with three low masts; and long narrow pinnaces arranged for many oars.

Timber, saw-mills, and new-cut planks spread in profusion around, and many of the town residences are seen to be adapted for warehouses and infirmaries.]

DUMB SHOW

Moving in this scene are countless companies of soldiery, engaged in a drill practice of embarking and disembarking, and of hoisting horses into the vessels and landing them again. Vehicles bearing provisions of many sorts load and unload before the temporary warehouses. Further off, on the open land, bodies of troops are at field-drill. Other bodies of soldiers, half stripped and encrusted with mud, are labouring as navvies in repairing the excavations.

An English squadron of about twenty sail, comprising a ship or two of the line, frigates, brigs, and luggers, confronts the busy spectacle from the sea.

The Show presently dims and becomes broken, till only its flashes and gleams are visible. Anon a curtain of cloud closes over it.

SCENE V

LONDON. THE HOUSE OF A LADY OF QUALITY

[A fashionable crowd is present at an evening party, which includes the DUKES of BEAUFORT and RUTLAND, LORDS MALMESBURY, HARROWBY, ELDON, GRENVILLE, CASTLEREAGH, SIDMOUTH, and MULGRAVE, with their ladies; also CANNING, PERCEVAL, TOWNSHEND, LADY ANNE HAMILTON, MRS. DAMER, LADY CAROLINE LAMB, and many other notables.]

A GENTLEMAN [offering his snuff-box]
So, then, the Treaty anxiously concerted
Between ourselves and frosty Muscovy
Is duly signed?

A CABINET MINISTER
Was signed a few days back,
And is in force. And we do firmly hope
The loud pretensions and the stunning dins
Now daily heard, these laudable exertions
May keep in curb; that ere our greening land
Darken its leaves beneath the Dogday suns,
The independence of the Continent
May be assured, and all the rumpled flags
Of famous dynasties so foully mauled,
Extend their honoured hues as heretofore.

GENTLEMAN
So be it. Yet this man is a volcano;
And proven 'tis, by God, volcanos choked
Have ere now turned to earthquakes!

LADY
What the news?—
The chequerboard of diplomatic moves
Is London, all the world knows: here are born
All inspirations of the Continent—
So tell!

GENTLEMAN
Ay. Inspirations now abound!

LADY
Nay, but your looks are grave! That measured speech
Betokened matter that will waken us.—
Is it some piquant cruelty of his?
Or other tickling horror from abroad
The packet has brought in?

GENTLEMAN
The treaty's signed!

MINISTER
Whereby the parties mutually agree
To knit in union and in general league
All outraged Europe.

LADY

So to knit sounds well;
But how ensure its not unravelling?

MINISTER
Well; by the terms. There are among them these:
Five hundred thousand active men in arms
Shall strike [supported by the Britannic aid
In vessels, men, and money subsidies]
To free North Germany and Hanover
From trampling foes; deliver Switzerland,
Unbind the galled republic of the Dutch,
Rethrone in Piedmont the Sardinian King,
Make Naples sword-proof, un-French Italy
From shore to shore; and thoroughly guarantee
A settled order to the divers states;
Thus rearing breachless barriers in each realm
Against the thrust of his usurping hand.

SPIRIT OF THE YEARS
They trow not what is shaping otherwhere
The while they talk this stoutly!

SPIRIT OF RUMOUR
Bid me go
And join them, and all blandly kindle them
By bringing, ere material transit can,
A new surprise!

SPIRIT OF THE YEARS
Yea, for a moment, wouldst.

[The Spirit of Rumour enters the apartment in the form of a personage of fashion, newly arrived. He advances and addresses the group.]

SPIRIT
The Treaty moves all tongues to-night.—Ha, well—
So much on paper!

GENTLEMAN
What on land and sea?
You look, old friend, full primed with latest thence.

SPIRIT
Yea, this. The Italy our mighty pact
Delivers from the French and Bonaparte
Makes haste to crown him!—Turning from Boulogne
He speeds toward Milan, there to glory him
In second coronation by the Pope,

And set upon his irrepressible brow
Lombardy's iron crown.

[The Spirit of Rumour mingles with the throng, moves away, and disappears.]

LADY
Fair Italy,
Alas, alas!

LORD
Yet thereby English folk
Are freed him.—Faith, as ancient people say,
It's an ill wind that blows good luck to none!

MINISTER
Who is your friend that drops so airily
This precious pinch of salt on our raw skin?

GENTLEMAN
Why, Norton. You know Norton well enough?

MINISTER
Nay, 'twas not he. Norton of course I know.
I thought him Stewart for a moment, but—-

LADY
But I well scanned him—'twas Lord Abercorn;
For, said I to myself, "O quaint old beau,
To sleep in black silk sheets so funnily:—
That is, if the town rumour on't be true."

LORD
My wig, ma'am, no! 'Twas a much younger man.

GENTLEMAN
But let me call him! Monstrous silly this,
That don't know my friends!

[They look around. The gentleman goes among the surging and babbling guests, makes inquiries, and returns with a perplexed look.]

GENTLEMAN
They tell me, sure,
That he's not here to-night!

MINISTER
I can well swear
It was not Norton.—'Twas some lively buck,

Who chose to put himself in masquerade
And enter for a whim. I'll tell our host.
—Meantime the absurdity of his report
Is more than manifested. How knows he
The plans of Bonaparte by lightning-flight,
Before another man in England knows?

LADY
Something uncanny's in it all, if true.
Good Lord, the thought gives me a sudden sweat,
That fairly makes my linen stick to me!

MINISTER
Ha-ha! 'Tis excellent. But we'll find out
Who this impostor was.

[They disperse, look furtively for the stranger, and speak of the incident to others of the crowded company.]

SPIRIT OF THE YEARS
Now let us vision onward, till we sight
Famed Milan's aisles of marble, sun-alight,
And there behold, unbid, the Coronation-rite.

[The confused tongues of the assembly waste away into distance, till they are heard but as the babblings of the sea from a high cliff, the scene becoming small and indistinct therewith. This passes into silence, and the whole disappears.]

SCENE VI

MILAN. THE CATHEDRAL

[The interior of the building on a sunny May day.

The walls, arched, and columns are draped in silk fringed with gold. A gilded throne stand in front of the High Altar. A closely packed assemblage, attired in every variety of rich fabric and fashion, waits in breathless expectation.]

DUMB SHOW

From a private corridor leading to a door in the aisle the EMPRESS JOSEPHINE enters, in a shining costume, and diamonds that collect rainbow-colours from the sunlight piercing the clerestory windows. She is preceded by PRINCESS ELIZA, and surrounded by her ladies. A pause follows, and then comes the procession of the EMPEROR, consisting of hussars, heralds, pages, aides-de-camp, presidents of institutions, officers of the state bearing the insignia of the Empire and of Italy, and seven ladies with offerings. The Emperor himself in royal robes, wearing the Imperial crown, and carrying the sceptre. He is followed my ministers and officials of the household. His gait is rather defiant than dignified, and a bluish pallor overspreads his face.

He is met by the Cardinal Archbishop of CAPRARA and the clergy, who burn incense before him as he proceeds towards the throne. Rolling notes of music burn forth, and loud applause from the congregation.

SPIRIT OF THE PITIES
What is the creed that these rich rites disclose?

SPIRIT OF THE YEARS
A local cult, called Christianity,
Which the wild dramas of the wheeling spheres
Include, with divers other such, in dim
Pathetical and brief parentheses,
Beyond whose span, uninfluenced, unconcerned,
The systems of the suns go sweeping on
With all their many-mortaled planet train
In mathematic roll unceasingly.

SPIRIT OF THE PITIES
I did not recognize it here, forsooth;
Though in its early, lovingkindly days
Of gracious purpose it was much to me.

ARCHBISHOP [addressing Bonaparte]
Sire, with that clemency and right goodwill
Which beautify Imperial Majesty,
You deigned acceptance of the homages
That we the clergy and the Milanese
Were proud to offer when your entrance here
Streamed radiance on our ancient capital.
Please, then, to consummate the boon to-day
Beneath this holy roof, so soon to thrill
With solemn strains and lifting harmonies
Befitting such a coronation hour;
And bend a tender fatherly regard
On this assembly, now at one with me
To supplicate the Author of All Good
That He endow your most Imperial person
With every Heavenly gift.

[The procession advances, and the EMPEROR seats himself on the throne, with the banners and regalia of the Empire on his right, and those of Italy on his left hand. Shouts and triumphal music accompany the proceedings, after which Divine service commences.]

SPIRIT OF THE PITIES
Thus are the self-styled servants of the Highest

Constrained by earthly duress to embrace
Mighty imperiousness as it were choice,
And hand the Italian sceptre unto one
Who, with a saturnine, sour-humoured grin,
Professed at first to flout antiquity,
Scorn limp conventions, smile at mouldy thrones,
And level dynasts down to journeymen!—
Yet he, advancing swiftly on that track
Whereby his active soul, fair Freedom's child
Makes strange decline, now labours to achieve
The thing it overthrew.

SPIRIT OF THE YEARS
Thou reasonest ever thuswise—even if
A self-formed force had urged his loud career.

SPIRIT SINISTER
Do not the prelate's accents falter thin,
His lips with inheld laughter grow deformed,
While blessing one whose aim is but to win
The golden seats that other b—s have warmed?

SPIRIT OF THE YEARS
Soft, jester; scorn not puppetry so skilled,
Even made to feel by one men call the Dame.

SHADE OF THE EARTH
Yea; that they feel, and puppetry remain,
Is an owned flaw in her consistency
Men love to dub Dame Nature—that lay-shape
They use to hang phenomena upon—
Whose deftest mothering in fairest sphere
Is girt about by terms inexorable!

SPIRIT SINISTER
The lady's remark is apposite, and reminds me that I may as well hold my tongue as desired. For if my casual scorn, Father Years, should set thee trying to prove that there is any right or reason in the Universe, thou wilt not accomplish it by Doomsday! Small blame to her, however; she must cut her coat according to her cloth, as they would say below there.

SPIRIT OF THE YEARS
O would that I could move It to enchain thee,
And shut thee up a thousand years!—[to cite
A grim terrestrial tale of one thy like]
Thou Iago of the Incorporeal World,
"As they would say below there."

SPIRIT OF THE PITIES

Would thou couldst!
But move That scoped above percipience, Sire,
It cannot be!

SHADE OF THE EARTH
The spectacle proceeds.

SPIRIT SINISTER
And we may as well give all attention thereto, for the evils at work in other continents are not worth
eyesight by comparison.

[The ceremonial in the Cathedral continues. NAPOLEON goes to the front of the altar, ascends the
steps, and, taking up the crown of Lombardy, places it on his head.]

NAPOLEON
'Tis God has given it to me. So be it.
Let any who shall touch it now beware! [Reverberations of applause.]

[The Sacrament of the Mass. NAPOLEON reads the Coronation Oath in a loud voice.]

HERALDS
Give ear! Napoleon, Emperor of the French
And King of Italy, is crowned and throned!

CONGREGATION
Long live the Emperor and King. Huzza!

[Music. The Te Deum.]

SPIRIT OF THE PITIES
That vulgar stroke of vauntery he displayed
In planting on his brow the Lombard crown,
Means sheer erasure of the Luneville pacts,
And lets confusion loose on Europe's peace
For many an undawned year! From this rash hour
Austria but waits her opportunity
By secret swellings of her armaments
To link her to his foes.—I'll speak to him.

[He throws a whisper into NAPOLEON'S ear.]

Lieutenant Bonaparte,
Would it not seemlier be to shut thy heart
To these unhealthy splendours?—helmet thee
For her thou swar'st-to first, fair Liberty?

NAPOLEON
Who spoke to me?

ARCHBISHOP
Not I, Sire. Not a soul.

NAPOLEON
Dear Josephine, my queen, didst call my name?

JOSEPHINE
I spoke not, Sire.

NAPOLEON
Thou didst not, tender spouse;
I know it. Such harsh utterance was not thine.
It was aggressive Fancy, working spells
Upon a mind o'erwrought!

[The service closes. The clergy advance with the canopy to the foot of the throne, and the procession forms to return to the Palace.]

SPIRIT OF THE YEARS
Officious sprite,
Thou art young, and dost not heed the Cause of things
Which some of us have inkled to thee here;
Else wouldst thou not have hailed the Emperor,
Whose acts do but outshape Its governing.

SPIRIT OF THE PITIES
I feel, Sire, as I must! This tale of Will
And Life's impulsion by Incognizance
I cannot take!

SPIRIT OF THE YEARS
Let me then once again
Show to thy sceptic eye the very streams
And currents of this all-inhering Power,
And bring conclusion to thy unbelief.

[The scene assumes the preternatural transparency before mentioned, and there is again beheld as it were the interior of a brain which seems to manifest the volitions of a Universal Will, of whose tissues the personages of the action form portion.]

SPIRIT OF THE PITIES
Enough. And yet for very sorriness
I cannot own the weird phantasma real!

SPIRIT OF THE YEARS
Affection ever was illogical.

SPIRIT IRONIC [aside]
How should the Sprite own to such logic—a mere juvenile— who only came into being in what the earthlings call their Tertiary Age!

[The scene changes. The exterior of the Cathedral takes the place of the interior, and the point of view recedes, the whole fabric smalling into distance and becoming like a rare, delicately carved alabaster ornament. The city itself sinks to miniature, the Alps show afar as a white corrugation, the Adriatic and the Gulf of Genoa appear on this and on that hand, with Italy between them, till clouds cover the panorama.]

ACT SECOND

SCENE I

THE DOCKYARD, GIBRALTAR

[The Rock is seen rising behind the town and the Alameda Gardens, and the English fleet rides at anchor in the Bay, across which the Spanish shore from Algeciras to Carnero Point shuts in the West. Southward over the Strait is the African coast.]

SPIRIT OF THE YEARS
Our migratory Proskenion now presents
An outlook on the storied Kalpe Rock,
As preface to the vision of the Fleets
Spanish and French, linked for fell purposings.

RECORDING ANGEL [reciting]
Their motions and manoeuvres, since the fame
Of Bonaparte's enthronment at Milan
Swept swift through Europe's dumbed communities,
Have stretched the English mind to wide surmise.
Many well-based alarms [which strange report
Much aggravates] as to the pondered blow,
Flutter the public pulse; all points in turn—
Malta, Brazil, Wales, Ireland, British Ind—
Being held as feasible for force like theirs,
Of lavish numbers and unrecking aim.

"Where, where is Nelson?" questions every tongue;—
"How views he so unparalleled a scheme?"
Their slow uncertain apprehensions ask.
"When Villeneuve puts to sea with all his force,
What may he not achieve, if swift his course!"

SPIRIT OF THE YEARS

I'll call in Nelson, who has stepped ashore
For the first time these thrice twelvemonths and more,
And with him one whose insight has alone
Pierced the real project of Napoleon.

[Enter NELSON and COLLINGWOOD, who pace up and down.]

SPIRIT OF THE PITIES
Note Nelson's worn-out features. Much has he
Suffered from ghoulish ghast anxiety!

NELSON
In short, dear Coll, the letter which you wrote me
Had so much pith that I was fain to see you;
For I am sure that you indeed divine
The true intent and compass of a plot
Which I have spelled in vain.

COLLINGWOOD
I weighed it thus:
Their flight to the Indies being to draw us off,
That and no more, and clear these coasts of us—
The standing obstacle to his device—
He cared not what was done at Martinique,
Or where, provided that the general end
Should not be jeopardized—that is to say,
The full-united squadron's quick return.—
Gravina and Villeneuve, once back to Europe,
Can straight make Ferrol, raise there the blockade,
Then haste to Brest, there to relieve Ganteaume,
And next with four-or five-and fifty sail
Bear down upon our coast as they see fit.—
I read they aim to strike at Ireland still,
As formerly, and as I wrote to you.

NELSON
So far your thoughtful and sagacious words
Have hit the facts. But 'tis no Irish bay
The villains aim to drop their anchors in;
My word for it: they make the Wessex shore,
And this vast squadron handled by Villeneuve
Is meant to cloak the passage of their strength,
Massed on those transports—we being kept elsewhere
By feigning forces.—Good God, Collingwood,
I must be gone! Yet two more days remain
Ere I can get away.—I must be gone!

COLLINGWOOD

Wherever you may go to, my dear lord,
You carry victory with you. Let them launch,
Your name will blow them back, as sou'west gales
The gulls that beat against them from the shore.

NELSON
Good Collingwood, I know you trust in me;
But ships are ships, and do not kindly come
Out of the slow docks of the Admiralty
Like wharfside pigeons when they are whistled for:—
And there's a damned disparity of force,
Which means tough work awhile for you and me!

[The Spirit of the Years whispers to NELSON.]

And I have warnings, warnings, Collingwood,
That my effective hours are shortening here;
Strange warnings now and then, as 'twere within me,
Which, though I fear them not, I recognize!...
However, by God's help, I'll live to meet
These foreign boasters; yea, I'll finish them;
And then—well, Gunner Death may finish me!

COLLINGWOOD
View not your life so gloomily, my lord:
One charmed, a needed purpose to fulfil!

NELSON
Ah, Coll. Lead bullets are not all that wound....
I have a feeling here of dying fires,
A sense of strong and deep unworded censure,
Which, compassing about my private life,
Makes all my public service lustreless
In my own eyes.—I fear I am much condemned
For those dear Naples and Palermo days,
And her who was the sunshine of them all!...
He who is with himself dissatisfied,
Though all the world find satisfaction in him,
Is like a rainbow-coloured bird gone blind,
That gives delight it shares not. Happiness?
It's the philosopher's stone no alchemy
Shall light on this world I am weary of.—
Smiling I'd pass to my long home to-morrow
Could I with honour, and my country's gain.
—But let's adjourn. I waste your hours ashore
By such ill-timed confessions!

[They pass out of sight, and the scene closes.]

SCENE II.

OFF FERROL

[The French and Spanish combined squadrons. On board the French admiral's flag-ship. VILLENEUVE is discovered in his cabin, writing a letter.]

SPIRIT OF THE PITIES
He pens in fits, with pallid restlessness,
Like one who sees Misfortune walk the wave,
And can nor face nor flee it.

SPIRIT OF THE YEARS
He indites
To his long friend the minister Decres
Words that go heavily!...

VILLENEUVE [writing]
"I am made the arbiter in vast designs
Whereof I see black outcomes. Do I this
Or do I that, success, that loves to jilt
Her anxious wooer for some careless blade,
Will not reward me. For, if I must pen it,
Demoralized past prayer in the marine—
Bad masts, bad sails, bad officers, bad men;
We cling to naval technics long outworn,
And time and opportunity do not avail me
To take up new. I have long suspected such,
But till I saw my helps, the Spanish ships,
I hoped somewhat.—Brest is my nominal port;
Yet if so, Calder will again attack—
Now reinforced by Nelson or Cornwallis—
And shatter my whole fleet.... Shall I admit
That my true inclination and desire
Is to make Cadiz straightway, and not Brest?
Alas! thereby I fail the Emperor;
But shame the navy less.—

"Your friend, VILLENEUVE"

[GENERAL LAURISTON enters.]

LAURISTON
Admiral, my missive to the Emperor,
Which I shall speed by special courier

From Ferrol this near eve, runs thus and thus:—
"Gravina's ships, in Ferrol here at hand,
Embayed but by a temporary wind,
Are all we now await. Combined with these
We sail herefrom to Brest; there promptly give
Cornwallis battle, and release Ganteaume;
Thence, all united, bearing Channelwards:
A step that sets in motion the first wheel
In the proud project of your Majesty
Now to be engined to the very close,
To wit: that a French fleet shall enter in
And hold the Channel four-and-twenty hours."—
Such clear assurance to the Emperor
That our intent is modelled on his will
I hasten to dispatch to him forthwith. (4)

VILLENEUVE
Yes, Lauriston. I sign to every word.

[Lauriston goes out. VILLENEUVE remains at his table in reverie.]

SPIRIT OF THE YEARS
We may impress him under visible shapes
That seem to shed a silent circling doom;
He's such an one as can be so impressed,
And this much is among our privileges,
Well bounded as they be.—Let us draw near him.

[The Spirits of Years and of the Pities take the form of sea-birds, which alight on the stern-balcony of
VILLENEUVE's ship, immediately outside his cabin window. VILLENEUVE after a while looks up and sees
the birds watching him with large piercing eyes.]

VILLENEUVE
My apprehensions even outstep their cause,
As though some influence smote through yonder pane.

[He gazes listlessly, and resumes his broodings.]

—Why dared I not disclose to him my thought,
As nightly worded by the whistling shrouds,
That Brest will never see our battled hulls
Helming to north in pomp of cannonry
To take the front in this red pilgrimage!
—If so it were, now, that I'd screen my skin
From risks of bloody business in the brunt,
My acts could scarcely wear a difference.
Yet I would die to-morrow—not ungladly—
So far removed is carcase-care from me.

For no self do these apprehensions spring,
But for the cause.—Yes, rotten is our marine,
Which, while I know, the Emperor knows not,
And the pale secret chills! Though some there be
Would beard contingencies and buffet all,
I'll not command a course so conscienceless.
Rather I'll stand, and face Napoleon's rage
When he shall learn what mean the ambiguous lines
That facts have forced from me.

SPIRIT OF THE PITIES [to the Spirit of Years]
O Eldest-born of the Unconscious Cause—
If such thou beest, as I can fancy thee—
Why dost thou rack him thus? Consistency
Might be preserved, and yet his doom remain.
His olden courage is without reproach;
Albeit his temper trends toward gaingiving!

SPIRIT OF THE YEARS
I say, as I have said long heretofore,
I know but narrow freedom. Feel'st thou not
We are in Its hand, as he?—Here, as elsewhere,
We do but as we may; no further dare.

[The birds disappear, and the scene is lost behind sea-mist.]

SCENE III

THE CAMP AND HARBOUR OF BOULOGNE

[The English coast in the distance. Near the Tour d'Ordre stands a hut, with sentinels and aides outside;
it is NAPOLEON's temporary lodging when not at his headquarters at the Chateau of Pont-de-Briques,
two miles inland.]

DUMB SHOW
A courier arrives with dispatches, and enters the Emperor's quarters, whence he emerges and goes on
with other dispatches to the hut of DECRES, lower down. Immediately after, NAPOLEON comes out
from his hut with a paper in his hand, and musingly proceeds towards an eminence commanding the
Channel.

Along the shore below are forming in a far-reaching line more than a hundred thousand infantry. On
the downs in the rear of the camps fifteen thousand cavalry are manoeuvring, their accoutrements
flashing in the sun like a school of mackerel. The flotilla lies in and around the port, alive with moving
figures.

With his head forward and his hands behind him the Emperor surveys these animated proceedings in detail, but more frequently turns his face toward the telegraph on the cliff to the southwest, erected to signal when VILLENEUVE and the combined squadrons shall be visible on the west horizon.

He summons one of the aides, who descends to the hut of DECRES. DECRES comes out from his hut, and hastens to join the Emperor. Dumb show ends.

[NAPOLEON and DECRES advance to the foreground of the scene.]

NAPOLEON
Decres, this action with Sir Robert Calder
Three weeks ago, whereof we dimly heard,
And clear details of which I have just unsealed,
Is on the whole auspicious for our plan.
It seems that twenty of our ships and Spain's—
None over eighty-gunned, and some far less—
Engaged the English off Cape Finisterre
With fifteen vessels of a hundred each.
We coolly fought and orderly as they,
And, but for mist, we had closed with victory.
Two English were much mauled, some Spanish damaged,
And Calder then drew off with his two wrecks
And Spain's in tow, we giving chase forthwith.
Not overtaking him our admiral,
Having the coast clear for his purposes,
Entered Coruna, and found order there
To open the port of Brest and come on hither.
Thus hastes the moment when the double fleet
Of Villeneuve and of Ganteaume should appear.

[He looks again towards the telegraph.]

DECRES [with hesitation]
And should they not appear, your Majesty?

NAPOLEON
Not? But they will; and do it early, too!
There's nothing hinders them. My God, they must,
For I have much before me when this stroke
At England's dealt. I learn from Talleyrand
That Austrian preparations threaten hot,
While Russia's hostile schemes are ripening,
And shortly must be met.—My plan is fixed:
I am prepared for each alternative.
If Villeneuve come, I brave the British coast,
Convulse the land with fear ['tis even now
So far distraught, that generals cast about
To find new modes of warfare; yea, design

Carriages to transport their infantry!].—
Once on the English soil I hold it firm,
Descend on London, and the while my men
Salute the dome of Paul's I cut the knot
Of all Pitt's coalitions; setting free
From bondage to a cold manorial caste
A people who await it.

[They stand and regard the chalky cliffs of England, till NAPOLEON resumes]:

Should it be
Even that my admirals fail to keep the tryst—
A thing scarce thinkable, when all's reviewed—
I strike this seaside camp, cross Germany,
With these two hundred thousand seasoned men,
And pause not till within Vienna's walls
I cry checkmate. Next, Venice, too, being taken,
And Austria's other holdings down that way,
The Bourbons also driven from Italy,
I strike at Russia—each in turn, you note,
Ere they can act conjoined.
Report to me
What has been scanned to-day upon the main,
And on your passage down request them there
To send Daru this way.

DECRES [as he withdraws]
The Emperor can be sanguine. Scarce can I.
His letters are more promising than mine.
Alas, alas, Villeneuve, my dear old friend,
Why do you pen me this at such a time!

[He retires reading VILLENEUVE'S letter. The Emperor walks up and down till DARU, his private
secretary, joins him.]

NAPOLEON
Come quick, Daru; sit down upon the grass,
And write whilst I am in mind.

First to Villeneuve:—

"I trust, Vice-Admiral, that before this date
Your fleet has opened Brest, and gone. If not,
These lines will greet you there. But pause not, pray:
Waste not a moment dallying. Sail away:
Once bring my coupled squadrons Channelwards
And England's soil is ours. All's ready here,
The troops alert, and every store embarked.

Hold the nigh sea but four-and-twenty hours
And our vast end is gained."

Now to Ganteaume:—

"My telegraphs will have made known to you
My object and desire to be but this,
That you forbid Villeneuve to lose an hour
In getting fit and putting forth to sea,
To profit by the fifty first-rate craft
Wherewith I now am bettered. Quickly weigh,
And steer you for the Channel with all your strength.
I count upon your well-known character,
Your enterprize, your vigour, to do this.
Sail hither, then; and we will be avenged
For centuries of despite and contumely."

DARU
Shall a fair transcript, Sire, be made forthwith?

NAPOLEON
This moment. And the courier will depart
And travel without pause.

[DARU goes to his office a little lower down, and the Emperor lingers on the cliffs looking through his glass.

The point of view shifts across the Channel, the Boulogne cliffs sinking behind the water-line.]

SCENE IV

SOUTH WESSEX. A RIDGE-LIKE DOWN NEAR THE COAST

[The down commands a wide view over the English Channel in front of it, including the popular Royal watering-place, with the Isle of Slingers and its roadstead, where men-of-war and frigates are anchored. The hour is ten in the morning, and the July sun glows upon a large military encampment round about the foreground, and warms the stone field-walls that take the place of hedges here.

Artillery, cavalry, and infantry, English and Hanoverian, are drawn up for review under the DUKE OF CUMBERLAND and officers of the staff, forming a vast military array, which extends three miles, and as far as the downs are visible.

In the centre by the Royal Standard appears KING GEORGE on horseback, and his suite. In a coach drawn by six cream-coloured Hanoverian horses, QUEEN CHARLOTTE sits with three Princesses; in another carriage with four horses are two more Princesses. There are also present with the Royal Party the LORD CHANCELLOR, LORD MULGRAVE, COUNT MUNSTER, and many other luminaries of fashion and influence.

The Review proceeds in dumb show; and the din of many bands mingles with the cheers. The turf behind the saluting-point is crowded with carriages and spectators on foot.]

A SPECTATOR
And you've come to the sight, like the King and myself? Well, one fool makes many. What a mampus o' folk it is here to-day! And what a time we do live in, between wars and wassailings, the goblin o' Boney, and King George in flesh and blood!

SECOND SPECTATOR
Yes. I wonder King George is let venture down on this coast, where he might be snapped up in a moment like a minney by a her'n, so near as we be to the field of Boney's vagaries! Begad, he's as like to land here as anywhere. Gloucester Lodge could be surrounded, and George and Charlotte carried off before he could put on his hat, or she her red cloak and pattens!

THIRD SPECTATOR
'Twould be so such joke to kidnap 'em as you think. Look at the frigates down there. Every night they are drawn up in a line across the mouth of the Bay, almost touching each other; and ashore a double line of sentinels, well primed with beer and ammunition, one at the water's edge and the other on the Esplanade, stretch along the whole front. Then close to the Lodge a guard is mounted after eight o'clock; there be pickets on all the hills; at the Harbour mouth is a battery of twenty four-pounders; and over-right 'em a dozen six-pounders, and several howitzers. And next look at the size of the camp of horse and foot up here.

FIRST SPECTATOR
Everybody however was fairly gallied this week when the King went out yachting, meaning to be back for the theatre; and the eight or nine o'clock came, and never a sign of him. I don't know when 'a did land; but 'twas said by all that it was a foolhardy pleasure to take.

FOURTH SPECTATOR
He's a very obstinate and comical old gentleman; and by all account 'a wouldn't make port when asked to.

SECOND SPECTATOR
Lard, Lard, if 'a were nabbed, it wouldn't make a deal of difference! We should have nobody to zing, and play singlestick to, and grin at through horse-collars, that's true. And nobody to sign our few documents. But we should rub along some way, goodnow.

FIRST SPECTATOR
Step up on this barrow; you can see better. The troopers now passing are the York Hussars—foreigners to a man, except the officers—the same regiment the two young Germans belonged to who were shot four years ago. Now come the Light Dragoons; what a time they take to get all past! Well, well! this day will be recorded in history.

SECOND SPECTATOR

Or another soon to follow it! [He gazes over the Channel.] There's not a speck of an enemy upon that shiny water yet; but the Brest fleet is zaid to have put to sea, to act in concert with the army crossing from Boulogne; and if so the French will soon be here; when God save us all! I've took to drinking neat, for, say I, one may as well have innerds burnt out as shot out, and 'tis a good deal pleasanter for the man that owns 'em. They say that a cannon-ball knocked poor Jim Popple's maw right up into the futtock-shrouds at the Nile, where 'a hung like a nightcap out to dry. Much good to him his obeying his old mother's wish and refusing his allowance o' rum!

[The bands play and the Review continues till past eleven o'clock. Then follows a sham fight. At noon precisely the royal carriages draw off the ground into the highway that leads down to the town and Gloucester Lodge, followed by other equipages in such numbers that the road is blocked. A multitude comes after on foot. Presently the vehicles manage to proceed to the watering-place, and the troops march away to the various camps as a sea-mist cloaks the perspective.]

SCENE V

THE SAME. RAINBARROW'S BEACON, EGDON HEATH

[Night in mid-August of the same summer. A lofty ridge of heathland reveals itself dimly, terminating in an abrupt slope, at the summit of which are three tumuli. On the sheltered side of the most prominent of these stands a hut of turves with a brick chimney. In front are two ricks of fuel, one of heather and furze for quick ignition, the other of wood, for slow burning.

Something in the feel of the darkness and in the personality of the spot imparts a sense of uninterrupted space around, the view by day extending from the cliffs of the Isle of Wight eastward to Blackdon Hill by Deadman's Bay westward, and south across the Valley of the Froom to the ridge that screens the Channel.

Two men with pikes loom up, on duty as beacon-keepers beside the ricks.]

OLD MAN
Now, Jems Purchess, once more mark my words. Black'on is the point we've to watch, and not Kingsbere; and I'll tell 'ee for why. If he do land anywhere hereabout 'twill be inside Deadman's Bay, and the signal will straightaway come from Black'on. But there thou'st stand, glowering and staring with all thy eyes at Kingsbere! I tell 'ee what 'tis, Jem Purchess, your brain is softening; and you be getting too old for business of state like ours!

YOUNG MAN
You've let your tongue wrack your few rames of good breeding, John.

OLD MAN
The words of my Lord-Lieutenant was, whenever you see Kingsbere-Hill Beacon fired to the eastward, or Black'on to the westward, light up; and keep your second fire burning for two hours. Was that our documents or was it not?

YOUNG MAN

I don't gainsay it. And so I keep my eye on Kingsbere because that's most likely o' the two, says I.

OLD MAN
That shows the curious depths of your ignorance. However, I'll have patience, and say on. Didst ever larn geography?

YOUNG MAN
No. Nor no other corrupt practices.

OLD MAN
Tcht-tcht!—Well, I'll have patience, and put it to him in another form. Dost know the world is round—eh? I warrant dostn't!

YOUNG MAN
I warrant I do!

OLD MAN
How d'ye make that out, when th'st never been to school?

YOUNG MAN
I larned it at church, thank God.

OLD MAN
Church? What have God A'mighty got to do with profane knowledge?
Beware that you baint blaspheming, Jems Purchess!

YOUNG MAN
I say I did, whether or no! 'Twas the zingers up in gallery that I had it from. They busted out that strong with "the round world and they that dwell therein," that we common fokes down under could do no less than believe 'em.

OLD MAN
Canst be sharp enough in the wrong place as usual—I warrant canst! However, I'll have patience with 'en and say on!—Suppose, now, my hat is the world; and there, as might be, stands the Camp of Belong, where Boney is. The world goes round, so, and Belong goes round too. Twelve hours pass; round goes the world still—so. Where's Belong now?

[A pause. Two other figures, a man's and a woman's, rise against the sky out of the gloom.]

OLD MAN [shouldering his pike]
Who goes there? Friend or foe, in the King's name!

WOMAN
Piece o' trumpery! "Who goes" yourself! What d'ye talk o', John Whiting! Can't your eyes earn their living any longer, then, that you don't know your own neighbours? 'Tis Private Cantle of the Locals and his wife Keziar, down at Bloom's-End—who else should it be!

OLD MAN [lowering his pike]

A form o' words, Mis'ess Cantle, no more; ordained by his Majesty's Gover'ment to be spoke by all we on sworn duty for the defence o' the country. Strict rank-and-file rules is our only horn of salvation in these times.—But, my dear woman, why ever have ye come lumpering up to Rainbarrows at this time o' night?

WOMAN
We've been troubled with bad dreams, owing to the firing out at sea yesterday; and at last I could sleep no more, feeling sure that sommat boded of His coming. And I said to Cantle, I'll ray myself, and go up to Beacon, and ask if anything have been heard or seen to-night. And here we be.

OLD MAN
Not a sign or sound—all's as still as a churchyard. And how is your good man?

PRIVATE [advancing]
Clk. I be all right! I was in the ranks, helping to keep the ground at the review by the King this week. We was a wonderful sight—wonderful! The King said so again and again.—Yes, there was he, and there was I, though not daring to move a' eyebrow in the presence of Majesty. I have come home on a night's leave—off there again to-morrow. Boney's expected every day, the Lord be praised! Yes, our hopes are to be fulfilled soon, as we say in the army.

OLD MAN
There, there, Cantle; don't ye speak quite so large, and stand so over-upright. Your back is as holler as a fire-dog's. Do ye suppose that we on active service here don't know war news? Mind you don't go taking to your heels when the next alarm comes, as you did at last year's.

PRIVATE
That had nothing to do with fighting, for I'm as bold as a lion when I'm up, and "Shoulder Fawlocks!" sounds as common as my own name to me. 'Twas—- [lowering his voice.] Have ye heard?

OLD MAN
To be sure we have.

PRIVATE
Ghastly, isn't it!

OLD MAN
Ghastly! Frightful!

YOUNG MAN [to Private]
He don't know what it is! That's his pride and puffery. What is it that' so ghastly—hey?

PRIVATE
Well, there, I can't tell it. 'Twas that that made the whole eighty of our company run away—though we be the bravest of the brave in natural jeopardies, or the little boys wouldn't run after us and call us and call us the "Bang-up-Locals."

WOMAN [in undertones]

I can tell you a word or two on't. It is about His victuals. They say that He lives upon human flesh, and has rashers o' baby every morning for breakfast—for all the world like the Cernal Giant in old ancient times!

YOUNG MAN
Ye can't believe all ye hear.

PRIVATE
I only believe half. And I only own—such is my challengeful character—that perhaps He do eat pagan infants when He's in the desert. But not Christian ones at home. Oh no—'tis too much.

WOMAN
Whether or no, I sometimes—God forgive me!—laugh wi' horror at the queerness o't, till I am that weak I can hardly go round the house. He should have the washing of 'em a few times; I warrant 'a wouldn't want to eat babies any more!

[A silence, during which they gaze around at the dark dome of the starless sky.]

YOUNG MAN
There'll be a change in the weather soon, by the look o't. I can hear the cows moo in Froom Valley as if I were close to 'em, and the lantern at Max Turnpike is shining quite plain.

OLD MAN
Well, come in and taste a drop o' sommat we've got here, that will warm the cockles of your heart as ye wamble homealong. We housed eighty tuns last night for them that shan't be named—landed at Lullwind Cove the night afore, though they had a narrow shave with the riding-officers this run.

[They make toward the hut, when a light on the west horizon becomes visible, and quickly enlarges.]

YOUNG MAN
He's come!

OLD MAN
Come he is, though you do say it! This, then, is the beginning of what England's waited for!

[They stand and watch the light awhile.]

YOUNG MAN
Just what you was praising the Lord for by-now, Private Cantle.

PRIVATE
My meaning was—-

WOMAN [simpering]
Oh that I hadn't married a fiery sojer, to make me bring fatherless children into the world, all through his dreadful calling! Why didn't a man of no sprawl content me!

OLD MAN [shouldering his pike]

We can't heed your innocent pratings any longer, good neighbours, being in the King's service, and a hot invasion on. Fall in, fall in, mate. Straight to the tinder-box. Quick march!

[The two men hasten to the hut, and are heard striking a flint and steel. Returning with a lit lantern they ignite a blaze. The private of the Locals and his wife hastily retreat by the light of the flaming beacon, under which the purple rotundities of the heath show like bronze, and the pits like the eye-sockets of a skull.]

SPIRIT SINISTER
This is good, and spells blood. [To the Chorus of the Years.] I assume that It means to let us carry out this invasion with pleasing slaughter, so as not to disappoint my hope?

SEMICHORUS I OF THE YEARS [aerial music]
We carry out? Nay, but should we
Ordain what bloodshed is to be it!

SEMICHORUS II
The Immanent, that urgeth all,
Rules what may or may not befall!

SEMICHORUS I
Ere systemed suns were globed and lit
The slaughters of the race were writ,

SEMICHORUS II
And wasting wars, by land and sea,
Fixed, like all else, immutably!

SPIRIT SINISTER
Well; be it so. My argument is that War makes rattling good history; but Peace is poor reading. So I back Bonaparte for the reason that he will give pleasure to posterity.

SPIRIT OF THE PITIES
Gross hypocrite!

CHORUS OF THE YEARS
We comprehend him not.

[The day breaks over the heathery upland, on which the beacon is still burning. The morning reveals the white surface of a highway which, coming from the royal watering-place beyond the hills, stretched towards the outskirts of the heath and passes away eastward.]

DUMB SHOW
Moving figures and vehicles dot the surface of the road, all progressing in one direction, away from the coast. In the foreground the shapes appear as those of civilians, mostly on foot, but many in gigs and tradesmen's carts and on horseback. When they reach an intermediate hill some pause and look back; others enter on the next decline landwards without turning their heads.

From the opposite horizon numerous companies of volunteers, in the local uniform of red with green facings, (5) are moving coastwards in companies; as are also irregular bodies of pikemen without uniform; while on the upper slopes of the downs towards the shore regiments of the line are visible, with cavalry and artillery; all passing over to the coast.

At a signal from the Chief Intelligences two Phantoms of Rumour enter on the highway in the garb of country-men.

FIRST PHANTOM [to Pedestrians]
Wither so fast, good neighbours, and before breakfast, too? Emptybellies be bad to vamp on.

FIRST PEDESTRIAN
He's landed west'ard, out by Abbot's Beach. And if you have property you'll save it and yourselves, as we are doing!

SECOND PEDESTRIAN
All yesterday the firing at Boulogne
Was like the seven thunders heard in Heaven
When the fierce angel spoke. So did he draw
Full-manned, flat-bottomed for the shallowest shore,
Dropped down to west, and crossed our frontage here.
Seen from above they specked the water-shine
As will a flight of swallows toward dim eve,
Descending on a smooth and loitering stream
To seek some eyot's sedge.

SECOND PHANTOM
We are sent to enlighten you and ease your soul.
Even now a courier canters to the port
To check the baseless scare.

FIRST PEDESTRIAN
These be inland men who, I warrant 'ee, don't know a lerret from a lighter! Let's take no heed of such, comrade; and hurry on!

FIRST PHANTOM
Will you not hear
That what was seen behind the midnight mist,
Their oar-blades tossing twinkles to the moon,
Was but a fleet of fishing-craft belated
By reason of the vastness of their haul?

FIRST PEDESTRIAN
Hey? And d'ye know it?—Now I look back to the top o' Rudgeway the folk seem as come to a pause there.—Be this true, never again do I stir my stumps for any alarm short of the Day of Judgment! Nine times has my rheumatical rest been broke in these last three years by hues and cries of Boney upon us. 'Od rot the feller; now he's made a fool of me once more, till my inside is like a wash-tub, what wi' being so gallied, and running so leery!—But how if you be one of the enemy, sent to sow these tares, so to

speak it, these false tidings, and coax us into a fancied safety? Hey, neighbours? I don't, after all, care for this story!

SECOND PEDESTRIAN
Onwards again!
If Boney's come, 'tis best to be away;
And if he's not, why, we've a holiday!

[Exeunt Pedestrians. The Spirits of Rumour vanish, while the scene seems to become involved in the smoke from the beacon, and slowly disappears. (6)]

ACT THIRD

SCENE I

BOULOGNE. THE CHATEAU AT PONT-DE-BRIQUES

[A room in the Chateau, which is used as the Imperial quarters. The EMPEROR NAPOLEON, and M. GASPARD MONGE, the mathematician and philosopher, are seated at breakfast.]

OFFICER
Monsieur the Admiral Decres awaits
A moment's audience with your Majesty,
Or now, or later.

NAPOLEON
Bid him in at once—
At last Villeneuve has raised the Brest blockade!

[Enter DECRES.]

What of the squadron's movements, good Decres?
Brest opened, and all sailing Channelwards,
Like swans into a creek at feeding-time?

DECRES
Such news was what I'd hoped, your Majesty,
To send across this daybreak. But events
Have proved intractable, it seems, of late;
And hence I haste in person to report
The featless facts that just have dashed my—

NAPOLEON [darkening]
Well?

DECRES

Sire, at the very juncture when the fleets
Sailed out from Ferrol, fever raged aboard
"L'Achille" and "l'Algeciras": later on,
Mischief assailed our Spanish comrades' ships;
Several ran foul of neighbours; whose new hurts,
Being added to their innate clumsiness,
Gave hap the upper hand; and in quick course
Demoralized the whole; until Villeneuve,
Judging that Calder now with Nelson rode,
And prescient of unparalleled disaster
If he pushed on in so disjoint a trim,
Bowed to the inevitable; and thus, perforce,
Leaving to other opportunity
Brest and the Channel scheme, with vast regret
Steered southward into Cadiz.

NAPOLEON [having risen from the table]
What!—Is, then,
My scheme of years to be disdained and dashed
By this man's like, a wretched moral coward,
Whom you must needs foist on me as one fit
For full command in pregnant enterprise!

MONGE [aside]
I'm one too many here! Let me step out
Till this black squall blows over. Poor Decres.
Would that this precious project, disinterred
From naval archives of King Louis' reign,
Had ever lingered fusting where 'twas found. (7)

[Exit Monge.]

NAPOLEON

To help a friend you foul a country's fame!—
Decres, not only chose you this Villeneuve,
But you have nourished secret sour opinions
Akin to his, and thereby helped to scathe
As stably based a project as this age
Has sunned to ripeness. Ever the French Marine
Have you decried, ever contrived to bring
Despair into the fleet! Why, this Villeneuve,
Your man, this rank incompetent, this traitor—
Of whom I asked no more than fight and lose,
Provided he detain the enemy—
A frigate is too great for his command!
what shall be said of one who, at a breath,
When a few casual sailors find them sick,

When falls a broken boom or slitten sail,
When rumour hints that Calder's tubs and Nelson's
May join, and bob about in company,
Is straightway paralyzed, and doubles back
On all his ripened plans!—
Bring him, ay, bodily; hale him out from Cadiz,
Compel him up the Channel by main force,
And, having doffed him his supreme command,
Give the united squadrons to Ganteaume!

DECRES
Your Majesty, while umbraged, righteously,
By an event my tongue dragged dry to tell,
Makes my hard situation over-hard
By your ascription to the actors in't
Of motives such and such. 'Tis not for me
To answer these reproaches, Sire, and ask
Why years-long mindfulness of France's fame
In things marine should win no confidence.
I speak; but am unable to convince!

True is it that this man has been my friend
Since boyhood made us schoolmates; and I say
That he would yield the heel-drops of his heart
With joyful readiness this day, this hour,
To do his country service. Yet no less
Is it his drawback that he sees too far.
And there are times, Sire, when a shorter sight
Charms Fortune more. A certain sort of bravery
Some people have—to wit, this same Lord Nelson—
Which is but fatuous faith in one's own star
Swoln to the very verge of childishness,
[Smugly disguised as putting trust in God,
A habit with these English folk]; whereby
A headstrong blindness to contingencies
Carries the actor on, and serves him well
In some nice issues clearer sight would mar.
Such eyeless bravery Villeneuve has not;
But, Sire, he is no coward.

NAPOLEON
Well, have it so!—What are we going to do?
My brain has only one wish—to succeed!

DECRES
My voice wanes weaker with you, Sire; is nought!
Yet these few words, as Minister of Marine,
I'll venture now.—My process would be thus:—

Our projects for a junction of the fleets
Being well-discerned and read by every eye
Through long postponement, England is prepared.
I would recast them. Later in the year
Form sundry squadrons of this massive one,
Harass the English till the winter time,
Then rendezvous at Cadiz; where leave half
To catch the enemy's eye and call their cruizers,
While rounding Scotland with the other half,
You make the Channel by the eastern strait,
Cover the passage of our army-boats,
And plant the blow.

NAPOLEON
And what if they perceive
Our Scottish route, and meet us eastwardly?

DECRES
I have thought of it, and planned a countermove;
I'll write the scheme more clearly and at length,
And send it hither to your Majesty.

NAPOLEON
Do so forthwith; and send me in Daru.

[Exit DECRES. Re-enter MONGE.]

Our breakfast, Monge, to-day has been cut short,
And these discussions on the ancient tongues
Wherein you shine, must yield to modern moils.
Nay, hasten not away; though feeble wills,
Incompetence, ay, imbecility,
In some who feign to serve the cause of France,
Do make me other than myself just now!—
Ah—here's Daru.

[DARU enters. MONGE takes his leave.]

Daru, sit down and write. Yes, here, at once,
This room will serve me now. What think you, eh?
Villeneuve has just turned tail and run to Cadiz.
So quite postponed—perhaps even overthrown—
My long-conned project against yonder shore
As 'twere a juvenile's snow-built device
But made for melting! Think of it, Daru,—
My God, my God, how can I talk thereon!
A plan well judged, well charted, well upreared,
To end in nothing!... Sit you down and write.

[NAPOLEON walks up and down, and resumes after a silence.]

Write this.—A volte-face 'tis indeed!—Write, write!

DARU [holding pen to paper]
I wait, your Majesty.

NAPOLEON
First Bernadotte—
Yes; "Bernadotte moves out from Hanover
Through Hesse upon Wurzburg and the Danube.—
Marmont from Holland bears along the Rhine,
And joins at Mainz and Wurzburg Bernadotte...

While these prepare their routes the army here
Will turn its back on Britain's tedious shore,
And, closing up with Augereau at Brest,
Set out full force due eastward....
By the Black forest feign a straight attack,
The while our purpose is to skirt its left,
Meet in Franconia Bernadotte and Marmont;
Traverse the Danube somewhat down from Ulm;
Entrap the Austrian column by their rear;
Surround them, cleave them; roll upon Vienna,
Where, Austria settled, I engage the Tsar,
While Massena detains in Italy
The Archduke Charles.

Foreseeing such might shape,
Each high-and by-way to the Danube hence
I have of late had measured, mapped, and judged;
Such spots as suit for depots chosen and marked;
Each regiment's daily pace and bivouac
Writ tablewise for ready reference;
All which itineraries are sent herewith."

So shall I crush the two gigantic sets
Upon the Empire, now grown imminent.
—Let me reflect.—First Bernadotte—-but nay,
The courier to Marmont must go first.
Well, well.—The order of our march from hence
I will advise.... My knock at George's door
With bland inquiries why his royal hand
Withheld due answer to my friendly lines,
And tossed the irksome business to his clerks,
Is thus perforce delayed. But not for long.
Instead of crossing, thitherward I tour

By roundabout contrivance not less sure!

DARU
I'll bring the writing to your Majesty.

[NAPOLEON and DARU go out severally.]

CHORUS OF THE YEARS [aerial music]
Recording Angel, trace
This bold campaign his thought has spun apace—
One that bids fair for immortality
Among the earthlings—if immortal deeds
May be ascribed to so extempory
And transient a race!
It will be called, in rhetoric and rhyme,
As son to sire succeeds,
A model for the tactics of all time;
"The Great Campaign of that so famed year Five,"
By millions of mankind not yet alive.

SCENE II

THE FRONTIERS OF UPPER AUSTRIA AND BAVARIA

[A view of the country from mid-air, at a point south of the River Inn, which is seen as a silver thread, winding northward between its junction with the Salza and the Danube, and forming the boundaries of the two countries. The Danube shows itself as a crinkled satin riband, stretching from left to right in the far background of the picture, the Inn discharging its waters into the larger river.]

DUMB SHOW

A vast Austrian army creeps dully along the mid-distance, in the detached masses and columns of a whitish cast. The columns insensibly draw nearer to each other, and are seen to be converging from the east upon the banks of the Inn aforesaid.

A RECORDING ANGEL [in recitative]
This movement as of molluscs on a leaf,
Which from our vantage here we scan afar,
Is one manoeuvred by the famous Mack
To countercheck Napoleon, still believed
To be intent on England from Boulogne,
And heedless of such rallies in his rear.
Mack's enterprise is now to cross Bavaria—
Beneath us stretched in ripening summer peace
As field unwonted for these ugly jars—

Outraged Bavaria, simmering in disquiet
At Munich down behind us, Isar-fringed,
And torn between his fair wife's hate of France
And his own itch to gird at Austrian bluff
For riding roughshod through his territory,
Wavers from this to that. The while Time hastes
The eastward streaming of Napoleon's host,
As soon we see.

The silent insect-creep of the Austrian columns towards the banks of the Inn continues to be seen till the
view fades to nebulousness and dissolves.

SCENE III

BOULOGNE. THE ST. OMER ROAD

[It is morning at the end of August, and the road stretches out of the town eastward.

The divisions of the "Army-for-England" are making preparations to march. Some portions are in
marching order. Bands strike up, and the regiments start on their journey towards the Rhine and
Danube. Bonaparte and his officers watch the movements from an eminence. The soldiers, as they
pace along under their eagles with beaming eyes, sing "Le Chant du Depart," and other martial songs,
shout "Vive l'Empereur!" and babble of repeating the days of Italy, Egypt, Marengo, and Hohenlinden.]

NAPOLEON
Anon to England!

CHORUS OF INTELLIGENCES [aerial music]
If Time's weird threads so weave!

[The scene as it lingers exhibits the gradual diminishing of the troops along the roads through the
undulating August landscape, till each column is seen but as a train of dust; and the disappearance of
each marching mass over the eastern horizon.]

ACT FOURTH

SCENE I

KING GEORGE'S WATERING-PLACE, SOUTH WESSEX

[A sunny day in autumn. A room in the red-brick royal residence know as Gloucester Lodge. (8)

At a front triple-lighted window stands a telescope on a tripod. Through the open middle sash is visible the crescent-curved expanse of the Bay as a sheet of brilliant translucent green, on which ride vessels of war at anchor. On the left hand white cliffs stretch away till they terminate in St. Aldhelm's Head, and form a background to the level water-line on that side. In the centre are the open sea and blue sky. A near headland rises on the right, surmounted by a battery, over which appears the remoter bald grey brow of the Isle of Slingers.

In the foreground yellow sands spread smoothly, whereon there are sundry temporary erections for athletic sports; and closer at hand runs an esplanade on which a fashionable crowd is promenading. Immediately outside the Lodge are companies of soldiers, groups of officers, and sentries.

Within the room the KING and PITT are discovered. The KING'S eyes show traces of recent inflammation, and the Minister has a wasted look.]

KING

Yes, yes; I grasp your reasons, Mr. Pitt,
And grant you audience gladly. More than that,
Your visit to this shore is apt and timely,
And if it do but yield you needful rest
From fierce debate, and other strains of office
Which you and I in common have to bear,
'Twill be well earned. The bathing is unmatched
Elsewhere in Europe,—see its mark on me!—
The air like liquid life.—But of this matter:
What argue these late movements seen abroad?
What of the country now the session's past;
What of the country, eh? and of the war?

PITT

The thoughts I have laid before your Majesty
Would make for this, in sum:—
That Mr. Fox, Lord Grenville, and their friends,
Be straightway asked to join. With Melville gone,
With Sidmouth, and with Buckinghamshire too,
The steerage of affairs has stood of late
Somewhat provisional, as you, sir, know,
With stop-gap functions thrust on offices
Which common weal can tolerate but awhile.
So, for the weighty reasons I have urged,
I do repeat my most respectful hope
To win your Majesty's ungrudged assent
To what I have proposed.

KING

But nothing, sure,
Has been more plain to all, dear Mr. Pitt,
Than that your own proved energy and scope
Is ample, without aid, to carry on

Our just crusade against the Corsican.
Why, then, go calling Fox and Grenville in?
Such helps we need not. Pray you think upon't,
And speak to me again.—We've had alarms
Making us skip like crackers at our heels,
That Bonaparte had landed close hereby.

PITT
Such rumours come as regularly as harvest.

KING
And now he has left Boulogne with all his host?
Was it his object to invade at all,
Or was his vast assemblage there a blind?

PITT
Undoubtedly he meant invasion, sir,
Had fortune favoured. He may try it yet.
And, as I said, could we but close with Fox—-

KING
But, but;—I ask, what is his object now?
Lord Nelson's Captain—Hardy—whose old home
Stands in a peaceful vale hard by us here—
Who came two weeks ago to see his friends,
I talked to in this room a lengthy while.
He says our navy still is in thick night
As to the aims by sea of Bonaparte
Now the Boulogne attempt has fizzled out,
And what he schemes afloat with Spain combined.
The "Victory" lay that fortnight at Spithead,
And Nelson since has gone aboard and sailed;
Yes, sailed again. The "Royal Sovereign" follows,
And others her. Nelson was hailed and cheered
To huskiness while leaving Southsea shore,
Gentle and simple wildly thronging round.

PITT
Ay, sir. Young women hung upon his arm,
And old ones blessed, and stroked him with their hands.

KING
Ah—you have heard, of course. God speed him, Pitt.

PITT
Amen, amen!

KING

I read it as a thing
Of signal augury, and one which bodes
Heaven's confidence in me and in my line,
That I should rule as King in such an age!...
Well, well.—So this new march of Bonaparte's
Was unexpected, forced perchance on him?

PITT

It may be so, your Majesty; it may.
Last noon the Austrian ambassador,
Whom I consulted ere I posted down,
Assured me that his latest papers word
How General Mack and eighty thousand men
Have made good speed across Bavaria
To wait the French and give them check at Ulm,
That fortress-frontier-town, entrenched and walled,
A place long chosen as a vantage-point
Whereon to encounter them as they outwind
From the blind shades and baffling green defiles
Of the Black Forest, worn with wayfaring.
Here Mack will intercept his agile foe
Hasting to meet the Russians in Bohemia,
And cripple him, if not annihilate.

Thus now, sir, opens out this Great Alliance
Of Russia, Austria, England, whereto I
Have lent my earnest efforts through long months,
And the realm gives her money, ships, and men.—
It claps a muffler round the Cock's steel spurs,
And leaves me sanguine on his overthrow.
But, then,—this coalition of resources
Demands a strong and active Cabinet
To aid your Majesty's directive hand;
And thus I urge again the said additions—
These brilliant intellects of the other side
Who stand by Fox. With us conjoined, they—-

KING

What, what, again—in face of my sound reasons!
Believe me, Pitt, you underrate yourself;
You do not need such aid. The splendid feat
Of banding Europe in a righteous cause
That you have achieved, so soon to put to shame
This wicked bombardier of dynasties
That rule by right Divine, goes straight to prove
We had best continue as we have begun,
And call no partners to our management.
To fear dilemmas horning up ahead

Is not your wont. Nay, nay, now, Mr. Pitt,
I must be firm. And if you love your King
You'll goad him not so rashly to embrace
This Fox-Grenville faction and its friends.
Rather than Fox, why, give me civil war!
Hey, what? But what besides?

PITT
I say besides, sir,... nothing!

[A silence.]

KING [cheerfully]
The Chancellor's here, and many friends of mine: Lady Winchelsea, Lord and Lady Chesterfield, Lady
Bulkeley, General Garth, and Mr. Phipps the oculist—not the least important to me. He is a worthy and
a skilful man. My eyes, he says, are as marvellously improved in durability as I know them to be in
power. I have arranged to go to-morrow with the Princesses, and the Dukes of Cumberland, Sussex, and
Cambridge [who are also here] for a ride on the Ridgeway, and through the Camp on the downs. You'll
accompany us there?

PITT
I am honoured by your Majesty's commands.

[PITT looks resignedly out of the window.]

What curious structure do I see outside, sir?

KING
It's but a stage, a type of all the world. The burgesses have arranged it in my honour. At six o'clock this
evening there are to be combats at single-stick to amuse the folk; four guineas the prize for the man
who breaks most heads. Afterward there is to be a grinning match through horse-collars—a very
humorous sport which I must stay here and witness; for I am interested in whatever entertains my
subjects.

PITT
Not one in all the land but knows it, sir.

KING
Now, Mr. Pitt, you must require repose;
Consult your own convenience then, I beg,
On when you leave.

PITT
I thank your Majesty.

[He departs as one whose purpose has failed, and the scene shuts.]

SCENE II

BEFORE THE CITY OF ULM

[A prospect of the city from the east, showing in the foreground a low-lying marshy country bounded in mid-distance by the banks of the Danube, which, bordered by poplars and willows, flows across the picture from the left to the Elchingen Bridge near the right of the scene, and is backed by irregular heights and terraces of espaliered vines. Between these and the river stands the city, crowded with old gabled houses and surrounded by walls, bastions, and a ditch, all the edifices being dominated by the nave and tower of the huge Gothic Munster.

On the most prominent of the heights at the back—the Michaelsberg—to the upper-right of the view, is encamped the mass of the Austrian army, amid half-finished entrenchments. Advanced posts of the same are seen south-east of the city, not far from the advanced corps of the French Grand-Army under SOULT, MARMONT, LANNES, NEY, and DUPONT, which occupy in a semicircle the whole breadth of the flat landscape in front, and extend across the river to higher ground on the right hand of the panorama.

Heavy mixed drifts of rain and snow are descending impartially on the French and on the Austrians, the downfall nearly blotting out the latter on the hills. A chill October wind wails across the country, and the poplars yield slantingly to the gusts.]

DUMB SHOW
Drenched peasants are busily at work, fortifying the heights of the Austrian position in the face of the enemy. Vague companies of Austrians above, and of the French below, hazy and indistinct in the thick atmosphere, come and go without apparent purpose near their respective lines.

Closer at hand NAPOLEON, in his familiar blue-grey overcoat, rides hither and thither with his marshals, haranguing familiarly the bodies of soldiery as he passes them, and observing and pointing out the disposition of the Austrians to his companions.

Thicker sheets of rain fly across as the murk of evening increases, which at length entirely obscures the prospect, and cloaks its bleared lights and fires.

SCENE III

ULM. WITHIN THE CITY

[The interior of the Austrian headquarters on the following morning. A tempest raging without.

GENERAL MACK, haggard and anxious, the ARCHDUKE FERDINAND, PRINCE SCHWARZENBERG, GENERAL JELLACHICH, GENERALS RIESC, BIBERBACH, and other field officers discovered, seated at a table with a map spread out before them. A wood fire blazes between tall andirons in a yawning fireplace. At every more than usually boisterous gust of wind the smoke flaps into the room.]

MACK

The accursed cunning of our adversary
Confounds all codes of honourable war,
Which ever have held as granted that the track
Of armies bearing hither from the Rhine—
Whether in peace or strenuous invasion—
Should pierce the Schwarzwald, and through Memmingen,
And meet us in our front. But he must wind
And corkscrew meanly round, where foot of man
Can scarce find pathway, stealing up to us
Thiefwise, by out back door! Nevertheless,
If English war-fleets be abreast Boulogne,
As these deserters tell, and ripe to land there,
It destines Bonaparte to pack him back
Across the Rhine again. We've but to wait,
And see him go.

ARCHDUKE
But who shall say if these bright tales be true?

MACK
Even then, small matter, your Imperial Highness;
The Russians near us daily, and must soon—
Ay, far within the eight days I have named—
Be operating to untie this knot,
If we hold on.

ARCHDUKE
Conjectures these—no more;
I stomach not such waiting. Neither hope
Has kernel in it. I and my cavalry
With caution, when the shadow fall to-night,
Can bore some hole in this engirdlement;
Outpass the gate north-east; join General Werneck,
And somehow cut our way Bohemia-wards:
Well worth the hazard, in our straitened case!

MACK [firmly]
The body of our force stays here with me.
And I am much surprised, your Highness, much,
You mark not how destructive 'tis to part!
If we wait on, for certain we should wait
In our full strength, compacted, undispersed
By such partition as your Highness plans.

SCHWARZENBERG
There's truth in urging we should not divide,
But weld more closely.—Yet why stay at all?
Methinks there's but one sure salvation left,

To wit, that we conjunctly march herefrom,
And with much circumspection, towards the Tyrol.
The subtle often rack their wits in vain—
Assay whole magazines of strategy—
To shun ill loomings deemed insuperable,
When simple souls by stumbling up to them
Find the grim shapes but air. But let use grant
That the investing French so ring us in
As to leave not a span for such exploit;
Then go we—throw ourselves upon their steel,
And batter through, or die!—
What say you, Generals? Speak your minds, I pray.

JELLACHICH
I favour marching out—the Tyrol way.

RIESC
Bohemia best! The route thereto is open.

ARCHDUKE
My course is chosen. O this black campaign,
Which Pitt's alarmed dispatches pricked us to,
All unforseeing! Any risk for me
Rather than court humiliation here!

[MACK has risen during the latter remarks, walked to the window, and looked out at the rain. He returns with an air of embarrassment.]

MACK [to Archduke]
It is my privilege firmly to submit
That your Imperial Highness undertake
No venturous vaulting into risks unknown.—
Assume that you, Sire, as you have proposed,
With your light regiments and the cavalry,
Detach yourself from us, to scoop a way
By circuits northwards through the Rauhe Alps
And Herdenheim, into Bohemia:
Reports all point that you will be attacked,
Enveloped, borne on to capitulate.
What worse can happen here?—
Remember, Sire, the Emperor deputes me,
Should such a clash arise as has arisen,
To exercise supreme authority.
The honour of our arms, our race, demands
That none of your Imperial Highness' line
Be pounded prisoner by this vulgar foe,
Who is not France, but an adventurer,
Imposing on that country for his gain.

ARCHDUKE
But it seems clear to me that loitering here
Is full as like to compass our surrender
As moving hence. And ill it therefore suits
The mood of one of my high temperature
To pause inactive while await me means
Of desperate cure for these so desperate ills!

[The ARCHDUKE FERDINAND goes out. A troubled, silence follows, during which the gusts call into the chimney, and raindrops spit on the fire.]

SCHWARZENBERG
The Archduke bears him shrewdly in this course.
We may as well look matters in the face,
And that we are cooped and cornered is most clear;
Clear it is, too, that but a miracle
Can work to loose us! I have stoutly held
That this man's three years' ostentatious scheme
To fling his army on the tempting shores
Of our Allies the English was a—well—
Scarce other than a trick of thimble-rig
To still us into false security.

JELLACHICH
Well, I know nothing. None needs list to me,
But, on the whole, to southward seems the course
For lunging, all in force, immediately.

[Another pause.]

SPIRIT SINISTER
The Will throws Mack again into agitation:
Ho-ho—what he'll do now!

SPIRIT OF THE PITIES
Nay, hard one, nay;
The clouds weep for him!

SPIRIT SINISTER
If he must;
And it's good antic at a vacant time!

[MACK goes restlessly to the door, and is heard pacing about the vestibule, and questioning the aides and other officers gathered there.]

A GENERAL
He wavers like this smoke-wreath that inclines

Or north, or south, as the storm-currents rule!

MACK [returning]
Bring that deserter hither once again.

[A French soldier is brought in, blindfolded and guarded. The
bandage is removed.]

Well, tell us what he says.

AN OFFICER [after speaking to the prisoner in French]
He still repeats
That the whole body of the British strength
Is even now descending on Boulogne,
And that self-preservation must, if need,
Clear us from Bonaparte ere many days,
Who momently is moving.

MACK
Still retain him.

[He walks to the fire, and stands looking into it. The soldier is taken out.]

JELLACHICH [bending over the map in argument with RIESC]
I much prefer our self-won information;
And if we have Marshal Soult at Landsberg here,
[Which seems to be truth, despite this man,]
And Dupont hard upon us at Albeck,
With Ney not far from Gunzburg; somewhere here,
Or further down the river, lurking Lannes,
Our game's to draw off southward—if we can!

MACK [turning]
I have it. This we'll do. You Jellachich,
Unite with Spangen's troops at Memmingen,
To fend off mischief there. And you, Riesc,
Will make your utmost haste to occupy
The bridge and upper ground at Elchingen,
And all along the left bank of the stream,
Till you observe whereon to concentrate
And sever their connections. I couch here,
And hold the city till the Russians come.

A GENERAL [in a low voice]
Disjunction seems of all expedients worst:
If any stay, then stay should every man,
Gather, inlace, and close up hip to hip,
And perk and bristle hedgehog-like with spines!

MACK
The conference is ended, friends, I say,
And orders will be issued here forthwith.

[Guns heard.]

AN OFFICER
Surely that's from the Michaelsberg above us?

MACK
Never care. Here we stay. In five more days
The Russians hail, and we regain our bays.

[Exeunt severally.]

SCENE IV

BEFORE ULM. THE SAME DAY

[A high wind prevails, and rain falls in torrents. An elevated terrace near Elchingen forms the foreground.]

DUMB SHOW
From the terrace BONAPARTE surveys and dictates operations against the entrenched heights of the Michaelsberg that rise in the middle distance on the right above the city. Through the gauze of descending waters the French soldiery can be discerned climbing to the attack under NEY.

They slowly advance, recede, re-advance, halt. A time of suspense follows. Then they are seen in a state of irregular movement, even confusion; but in the end they carry the heights with the bayonet.

Below the spot whereon NAPOLEON and his staff are gathered, glistening wet and plastered with mud, obtrudes on the left the village of Elchingen, now in the hands of the French. Its white-walled monastery, its bridge over the Danube, recently broken by the irresistible NEY, wear a desolated look, and the stream, which is swollen by the rainfall and rasped by the storm, seems wanly to sympathise.

Anon shells are dropped by the French from the summits they have gained into the city below. A bomb from an Austrian battery falls near NAPOLEON, and in bursting raises a fountain of mud. The Emperor retreats with his officers to a less conspicuous station.

Meanwhile LANNES advances from a position near NAPOLEON till his columns reach the top of the Frauenberg hard by. The united corps of LANNES and NEY descend on the inner slope of the heights towards the city walls, in the rear of the retreating Austrians. One of the French columns scales a bastion, but NAPOLEON orders the assault to be discontinued, and with the wane of day the spectacle disappears.

SCENE V

THE SAME. THE MICHAELSBERG

[A chilly but rainless noon three days later. At the back of the scene, northward, rise the Michaelsberg heights; below stretches the panorama of the city and the Danube. On a secondary eminence forming a spur of the upper hill, a fire of logs is burning, the foremost group beside it being NAPOLEON and his staff, the former in his shabby greatcoat and plain turned-up hat, walking to and fro with his hands behind him, and occasionally stopping to warm himself. The French infantry are drawn up in a dense array at the back of these.

The whole Austrian garrison of Ulm marches out of the city gate opposite NAPOLEON. GENERAL MACK is at the head, followed by GIULAY, GOTTESHEIM, KLINAU, LICHTENSTEIN, and many other officers, who advance to BONAPARTE and deliver their swords.]

MACK
Behold me, Sire. Mack the unfortunate!

NAPOLEON
War, General, ever has its ups and downs,
And you must take the better and the worse
As impish chance or destiny ordains.
Come near and warm you here. A glowing fire
Is life on the depressing, mired, moist days
Of smitten leaves down-dropping clammily,
And toadstools like the putrid lungs of men.
[To his Lieutenants.] Cause them so stand to right and left of me.

[The Austrian officers arrange themselves as directed, and the body of the Austrians now file past their Conqueror, laying down their arms as they approach; some with angry gestures and words, others in moody silence.]

Listen, I pray you, Generals gathered her.
I tell you frankly that I know not why
Your master wages this wild war with me.
I know not what he seeks by such injustice,
Unless to give me practice in my trade—
That of a soldier—whereto I was bred:
Deemed he my craft might slip from me, unplied?
Let him now own me still a dab therein!

MACK
Permit me, your Imperial Majesty,
To speak one word in answer; which is this,
No war was wished for by my Emperor:
Russia constrained him to it!

NAPOLEON
If that be,
You are no more a European power.—
I would point out to him that my resources
Are not confined to these my musters here;
My prisoners of war, in route for France,
Will see some marks of my resources there!
Two hundred thousand volunteers, right fit,
Will join my standards at a single nod,
And in six weeks prove soldiers to the bone,
Whilst you recruits, compulsion's scavengings,
Scarce weld to warriors after toilsome years.

But I want nothing on this Continent:
The English only are my enemies.
Ships, colonies, and commerce I desire,
Yea, therewith to advantage you as me.
Let me then charge your Emperor, my brother,
To turn his feet the shortest way to peace.—
All states must have an end, the weak, the strong;
Ay; even may fall the dynasty of Lorraine!

[The filing past and laying down of arms by the Austrian army continues with monotonous regularity, as if it would never end.]

NAPOLEON [in a murmur, after a while]
Well, what cares England! She has won her game;
I have unlearnt to threaten her from Boulogne....

Her gold it is that forms the weft of this
Fair tapestry of armies marshalled here!
Likewise of Russia's drawing steadily nigh.
But they may see what these see, by and by.

SPIRIT OF THE YEARS
So let him speak, the while we clearly sight him
Moved like a figure on a lantern-slide.
Which, much amazing uninitiate eyes,
The all-compelling crystal pane but drags
Wither the showman wills.

SPIRIT IRONIC
And yet, my friend,
The Will itself might smile at this collapse
Of Austria's men-at-arms, so drolly done;
Even as, in your phantasmagoric show,
The deft manipulator of the slide

Might smile at his own art.

CHORUS OF THE YEARS [aerial music]
Ah, no: ah, no!
It is impassible as glacial snow.—
Within the Great Unshaken
These painted shapes awaken
A lesser thrill than doth the gentle lave
Of yonder bank by Danube's wandering wave
Within the Schwarzwald heights that give it flow!

SPIRIT OF THE PITIES
But O, the intolerable antilogy
Of making figments feel!

SPIRIT IRONIC
Logic's in that.
It does not, I must own, quite play the game.

CHORUS OF IRONIC SPIRITS [aerial music]
And this day wins for Ulm a dingy fame,
Which centuries shall not bleach from her name!

[The procession of Austrians continues till the scene is hidden by haze.]

SCENE VI

LONDON. SPRING GARDENS

[Before LORD MALMESBURY'S house, on a Sunday morning in the same autumn. Idlers pause and gather in the background.

PITT enters, and meets LORD MULGRAVE.]

MULGRAVE
Good day, Pitt. Ay, these leaves that skim the ground
With withered voices, hint that sunshine-time
Is well-nigh past.—And so the game's begun
Between him and the Austro-Russian force,
As second movement in the faceabout
From Boulogne shore, with which he has hocussed us?—
What has been heard on't? Have they clashed as yet?

PITT
The Emperor Francis, partly at my instance,
Has thrown the chief command on General Mack,

A man most capable and far of sight.
He centres by the Danube-bank at Ulm,
A town well-walled, and firm for leaning on
To intercept the French in their advance
From the Black Forest toward the Russian troops
Approaching from the east. If Bonaparte
Sustain his marches at the break-neck speed
That all report, they must have met ere now.
—There is a rumour... quite impossible!...

MULGRAVE
You still have faith in Mack as strategist?
There have been doubts of his far-sightedness.

PITT [hastily]
I know, I know.—I am calling here at Malmesbury's
At somewhat an unceremonious time
To ask his help to translate this Dutch print
The post has brought. Malmesbury is great at Dutch,
Learning it long at Leyden, years ago.

[He draws a newspaper from his pocket, unfolds it, and glances
it down.]

There's news here unintelligible to me
Upon the very matter! You'll come in?

[They call at LORD MAMESBURY'S. He meets them in the hall, and welcomes them with an
apprehensive look of foreknowledge.]

PITT
Pardon this early call. The packet's in,
And wings me this unreadable Dutch paper,
So, as the offices are closed to-day,
I have brought it round to you.

[Handling the paper.]

What does it say?
For God's sake, read it out. You know the tongue.

MALMESBURY [with hesitation]
I have glanced it through already—more than once—
A copy having reached me, too, by now...
We are in the presence of a great disaster!
See here. It says that Mack, enjailed in Ulm
By Bonaparte—from four side shutting round—
Capitulated, and with all his force

Laid down his arms before his conqueror!

[PITT's face changes. A silence.]

MULGRAVE
Outrageous! Ignominy unparalleled!

PITT
By God, my lord, these statement must be false!
These foreign prints are trustless as Cheap Jack
Dumfounding yokels at a country fair.
I heed no word of it.—Impossible.
What! Eighty thousand Austrians, nigh in touch
With Russia's levies that Kutuzof leads,
To lay down arms before the war's begun?
'Tis too much!

MALMESBURY
But I fear it is too true!
Note the assevered source of the report—
One beyond thought of minters of mock tales.
The writer adds that military wits
Cry that the little Corporal now makes war
In a new way, using his soldiers' legs
And not their arms, to bring him victory.
Ha-ha! The quip must sting the Corporal's foes.

PITT [after a pause]
O vacillating Prussia! Had she moved,
Had she but planted one foot firmly down,
All this had been averted.—I must go.
'Tis sure, 'tis sure, I labour but in vain!

[MALMESBURY accompanies him to the door, and PITT walks away disquietedly towards Whitehall, the other two regarding him as he goes.]

MULGRAVE
Too swiftly he declines to feebleness,
And these things well might shake a stouter frame!

MALMESBURY
Of late the burden of all Europe's cares,
Of hiring and maintaining half her troops,
His single pair of shoulders has upborne,
Thanks to the obstinacy of the King.—
His thin, strained face, his ready irritation,
Are ominous signs. He may not be for long.

MULGRAVE
He alters fast, indeed,—as do events.

MALMESBURY
His labour's lost; and all our money gone!
It looks as if this doughty coalition
On which we have lavished so much pay and pains
Would end in wreck.

MULGRAVE
All is not over yet;
The gathering Russian forces are unbroke.

MALMESBURY
Well; we shall see. Should Boney vanquish these,
And silence all resistance on that side,
His move will then be backward to Boulogne,
And so upon us.

MULGRAVE
Nelson to our defence!

MALMESBURY
Ay; where is Nelson? Faith, by this time
He may be sodden; churned in Biscay swirls;
Or blown to polar bears by boreal gales;
Or sleeping amorously in some calm cave
On the Canaries' or Atlantis' shore
Upon the bosom of his Dido dear,
For all that we know! Never a sound of him
Since passing Portland one September day—
To make for Cadiz; so 'twas then believed.

MULGRAVE
He's staunch. He's watching, or I am much deceived.

[MULGRAVE departs. MALMESBURY goes within. The scene shuts.]

ACT FIFTH

SCENE I

OFF CAPE TRAFALGAR

[A bird's eye view of the sea discloses itself. It is daybreak, and the broad face of the ocean is fringed on its eastern edge by the Cape and the Spanish shore. On the rolling surface immediately beneath the eye, ranged more or less in two parallel lines running north and south, one group from the twain standing off somewhat, are the vessels of the combined French and Spanish navies, whose canvases, as the sun edges upward, shine in its rays like satin.

On the western horizon two columns of ships appear in full sail, small as moths to the aerial vision. They are bearing down towards the combined squadrons.]

RECORDING ANGEL I [intoning from his book]
At last Villeneuve accepts the sea and fate,
Despite the Cadiz council called of late,
Whereat his stoutest captains—men the first
To do all mortals durst—
Willing to sail, and bleed, and bear the worst,
Short of cold suicide, did yet opine
That plunging mid those teeth of treble line
In jaws of oaken wood
Held open by the English navarchy
With suasive breadth and artful modesty,
Would smack of purposeless foolhardihood.

RECORDING ANGEL II
But word came, writ in mandatory mood,
To put from Cadiz, gain Toulon, and straight
At a said sign on Italy operate.
Moreover that Villeneuve, arrived as planned,
Would find Rosily in supreme command.—
Gloomy Villeneuve grows rash, and, darkly brave,
Leaps to meet war, storm, Nelson—even the grave.

SEMICHORUS I OF THE YEARS [aerial music]
Ere the concussion hurtle, draw abreast
Of the sea.

SEMICHORUS II
Where Nelson's hulls are rising from the west,
Silently.

SEMICHORUS I
Each linen wing outspread, each man and lad
Sworn to be

SEMICHORUS II
Amid the vanmost, or for Death, or glad
Victory!

[The point of sight descends till it is near the deck of the "Bucentaure," the flag-ship of VILLENEUVE. Present thereupon are the ADMIRAL, his FLAG-CAPTAIN MAGENDIE, LIEUTENANT DAUDIGNON, other naval officers and seamen.]

MAGENDIE
All night we have read their signals in the air,
Whereby the peering frigates of their van
Have told them of our trend.

VILLENEUVE
The enemy
Makes threat as though to throw him on our stern:
Signal the fleet to wear; bid Gravina
To come in from manoeuvring with his twelve,
And range himself in line.

[Officers murmur.]

I say again
Bid Gravina draw hither with his twelve,
And signal all to wear!—and come upon
The larboard tack with every bow anorth!—
So we make Cadiz in the worst event.
And patch our rags up there. As we head now
Our only practicable thoroughfare
Is through Gibraltar Strait—a fatal door!

Signal to close the line and leave no gaps.
Remember, too, what I have already told:
Remind them of it now. They must not pause
For signallings from me amid a strife
Whose chaos may prevent my clear discernment,
Or may forbid my signalling at all.
The voice of honour then becomes the chief's;
Listen they thereto, and set every stitch
To heave them on into the fiercest fight.
Now I will sum up all: heed well the charge;
EACH CAPTAIN, PETTY OFFICER, AND MAN
IS ONLY AT HIS POST WHEN UNDER FIRE.

[The ships of the whole fleet turn their bows from south to north as directed, and close up in two parallel curved columns, the concave side of each column being towards the enemy, and the interspaces of the first column being, in general, opposite the hulls of the second.]

AN OFFICER [straining his eyes towards the English fleet]
How they skip on! Their overcrowded sail
Bulge like blown bladders in a tripeman's shop
The market-morning after slaughterday!

PETTY OFFICER
It's morning before slaughterday with us,
I make so bold to bode!

[The English Admiral is seen to be signalling to his fleet. The signal is: "ENGLAND EXPECTS EVERY MAN TO DO HIS DUTY." A loud cheering from all the English ships comes undulating on the wind when the signal is read.]

VILLENEUVE
They are signalling too—Well, business soon begins!
You will reserve your fire. And be it known
That we display no admirals' flags at all
Until the action's past. 'Twill puzzle them,
And work to our advantage when we close.—
Yes, they are double-ranked, I think, like us;
But we shall see anon.

MAGENDIE
The foremost one
Makes for the "Santa Ana." In such case
The "Fougueux" might assist her.

VILLENEUVE
Be it so—
There's time enough.—Our ships will be in place,
And ready to speak back in iron words
When theirs cry Hail! in the same sort of voice.

[They prepare to receive the northernmost column of the enemy's ships headed by the "Victory," trying the distance by an occasional single shot. During their suspense a discharge is heard southward, and turning they behold COLLINGWOOD at the head of his column in the "Royal Sovereign," just engaging with the Spanish "Santa Ana." Meanwhile the "Victory's" mizzen-topmast, with spars and a quantity of rigging, is seen to have fallen, her wheel to be shot away, and her deck encumbered with dead and wounded men.]

VILLENEUVE
'Tis well! But see; their course is undelayed,
And still they near in clenched audacity!

DAUDIGNON
Which aim deft Lucas o' the "Redoubtable"
Most gallantly bestirs him to outscheme.—
See, how he strains, that on his timbers fall
Blows that were destined for his Admiral!

[During this the French ship "Redoubtable" is moving forward to interpose itself between the approaching "Victory" and the "Bucentaure."]

VILLENEUVE
Now comes it! The "Santisima Trinidad,"
The old "Redoubtable's" hard sides, and ours,
Will take the touse of this bombastic blow.
Your grapnels and your boarding-hatchets—ready!
We'll dash our eagle on the English deck,
And swear to fetch it!

CREW
Ay! We swear. Huzza
Long live the Emperor!

[But the "Victory" suddenly swerves to the rear of the "Bucentaure," and crossing her stern-waters, discharges a broadside into her and the "Redoubtable" endwise, wrapping the scene in folds of smoke. The point of view changes.]

SCENE II

THE SAME. THE QUARTER-DECK OF THE "VICTORY"

[The van of each division of the English fleet has drawn to the windward side of the combined fleets of the enemy, and broken their order, the "Victory" being now parallel to and alongside the "Redoubtable," the "Temeraire" taking up a station on the other side of that ship. The "Bucentaure" and the "Santisima Trinidad" become jammed together a little way ahead. A smoke and din of cannonading prevail, amid which the studding-sail booms are shot away.

NELSON, HARDY, BLACKWOOD, SECRETARY SCOTT, LIEUTENANT PASCO, BURKE the Purser, CAPTAIN ADAIR of the Marines, and other officers are on or near the quarter-deck.]

NELSON
See, there, that noble fellow Collingwood,
How straight he helms his ship into the fire!—
Now you'll haste back to yours [to BLACKWOOD].
—We must henceforth
Trust to the Great Disposer of events,
And justice of our cause!...

[BLACKWOOD leaves. The battle grows hotter. A double-headed shot cuts down seven or eight marines on the "Victory's" poop.]

Captain Adair, part those marines of yours,
And hasten to disperse them round the ship.—
Your place is down below, Burke, not up here;
Ah, yes; like David you would see the battle!

[A heavy discharge of musket-shot comes from the tops of the "Santisima Trinidad. ADAIR and PASCO fall. Another swathe of Marines is mowed down by chain-shot.]

SCOTT
My lord, I use to you the utmost prayers
That I have privilege to shape in words:
Remove your stars and orders, I would beg;
That shot was aimed at you.

NELSON
They were awarded to me as an honour,
And shall I do despite to those who prize me,
And slight their gifts? No, I will die with them,
If die I must.

[He walks up and down with HARDY.]

HARDY
At least let's put you on
Your old greatcoat, my lord—[the air is keen.].—
'Twill cover all. So while you still retain
Your dignities, you baulk these deadly aims

NELSON
Thank 'ee, good friend. But no,—I haven't time,
I do assure you—not a trice to spare,
As you well will see.

[A few minutes later SCOTT falls dead, a bullet having pierced his skull. Immediately after a shot passes between the Admiral and the Captain, tearing the instep of Hardy's shoe, and striking away the buckle. They shake off the dust and splinters it has scattered over them. NELSON glances round, and perceives what has happened to his secretary.]

NELSON
Poor Scott, too, carried off! Warm work this, Hardy;
Too warm to go on long.

HARDY
I think so, too;
Their lower ports are blocked against our hull,
And our charge now is less. Each knock so near
Sets their old wood on fire.

NELSON
Ay, rotten as peat.
What's that? I think she has struck, or pretty nigh!

[A cracking of musketry.]

HARDY
Not yet.—Those small-arm men there, in her tops,
Thin our crew fearfully. Now, too, our guns
Have dipped full down, or they would rake
The "Temeraire" there on the other side.

NELSON
True.—While you deal good measure out to these,
Keep slapping at those giants over here—
The "Trinidad," I mean, and the "Bucentaure,"
To win'ard—swelling up so pompously.

HARDY
I'll see no slackness shall be shown that way.

[They part and go in their respective directions. Gunners, naked to the waist and reeking with sweat,
are now in swift action on the several decks, and firemen carry buckets of water hither and thither. The
killed and wounded thicken around, and are being lifted and examined by the surgeons. NELSON and
HARDY meet again.]

NELSON
Bid still the firemen bring more bucketfuls,
And dash the water into each new hole
Our guns have gouged in the "Redoubtable,"
Or we shall all be set ablaze together.

HARDY
Let me once more advise, entreat, my lord,
That you do not expose yourself so clearly.
Those fellows in the mizzen-top up there
Are peppering round you quite perceptibly.

NELSON
Now, Hardy, don't offend me. They can't aim;
They only set their own rent sails on fire.—
But if they could, I would not hide a button
To save ten lives like mine. I have no cause
To prize it, I assure 'ee.—Ah, look there,
One of the women hit,—and badly, too.
Poor wench! Let some one shift her quickly down.

HARDY
My lord, each humblest sojourner on the seas,
Dock-labourer, lame longshore-man, bowed bargee,
Sees it as policy to shield his life
For those dependent on him. Much more, then,
Should one upon whose priceless presence here

Such issues hang, so many strivers lean,
Use average circumspection at an hour
So critical for us all.

NELSON
Ay, ay. Yes, yes;
I know your meaning, Hardy,; and I know
That you disguise as frigid policy
What really is your honest love of me.
But, faith, I have had my day. My work's nigh done;
I serve all interests best by chancing it
Here with the commonest.—Ah, their heavy guns
Are silenced every one! Thank God for that.

HARDY
'Tis so. They only use their small arms now.

[He goes to larboard to see what is progressing on that side between his ship and the "Santisima Trinidad."]

OFFICER [to seaman]
Swab down these stairs. The mess of blood about
Makes 'em so slippery that one's like to fall
In carrying the wounded men below.

[While CAPTAIN HARDY is still a little way off, LORD NELSON turns to walk aft, when a ball from one of the muskets in the mizzen-top of the "Redoubtable" enters his left shoulder. He falls upon his face on the deck. HARDY looks round, and sees what has happened.]

HARDY [hastily]
Ah—what I feared, and strove to hide I feared!...

[He goes towards NELSON, who in the meantime has been lifted by SERGEANT-MAJOR SECKER and two seamen.]

NELSON
Hardy, I think they've done for me at last!

HARDY
I hope not!

NELSON
Yes. My backbone is shot through.
I have not long to live.

[The men proceed to carry him below.]

Those tiller ropes

They've torn away, get instantly repaired!

[At sight of him borne along wounded there is great agitation among the crew.]

Cover my face. There will be no good be done
By drawing their attention off to me.
Bear me along, good fellows; I am but one
Among the many darkened here to-day!

[He is carried on to the cockpit over the crowd of dead and wounded.]

Doctor, I'm gone. I am waste o' time to you.

HARDY [remaining behind]
Hills, go to Collingwood and let him know
That we've no Admiral here.

[He passes on.]

A LIEUTENANT
Now quick and pick him off who did the deed—
That white-bloused man there in the mizzen-top.

POLLARD, a midshipman [shooting]
No sooner said than done. A pretty aim!

[The Frenchman falls dead upon the poop.

The spectacle seems now to become enveloped in smoke, and the point of view changes.]

SCENE III

THE SAME. ON BOARD THE "BUCENTAURE"

[The bowsprit of the French Admiral's ship is stuck fast in the stern-gallery of the "Santisima Trinidad,"
the starboard side of the "Bucentaure" being shattered by shots from two English three-deckers which
are pounding her on that hand. The poop is also reduced to ruin by two other English ships that are
attacking her from behind.

On the quarter-deck are ADMIRAL VILLENEUVE, the FLAG-CAPTAIN MAGENDIE, LIEUTENANTS
DAUDIGNON, FOURNIER, and others, anxiously occupied. The whole crew is in desperate action of
battle and stumbling among the dead and dying, who have fallen too rapidly to be carried below.]

VILLENEUVE
We shall be crushed if matters go on thus.—
Direct the "Trinidad" to let her drive,

That this foul tangle may be loosened clear!

DAUDIGNON
It has been tried, sir; but she cannot move.

VILLENEUVE
Then signal to the "Hero" that she strive
Once more to drop this way.

MAGENDIE
We may make signs,
But in the thickened air what signal's marked?—
'Tis done, however.

VILLENEUVE
The "Redoubtable"
And "Victory" there,—they grip in dying throes!
Something's amiss on board the English ship.
Surely the Admiral's fallen?

A PETTY OFFICER
Sir, they say
That he was shot some hour, or half, ago.—
With dandyism raised to godlike pitch
He stalked the deck in all his jewellery,
And so was hit.

MAGENDIE
Then Fortune shows her face!
We have scotched England in dispatching him. [He watches.]
Yes! He commands no more; and Lucas, joying,
Has taken steps to board. Look, spars are laid,
And his best men are mounting at his heels.

VILLENEUVE
Ah, God—he is too late! Whence came the hurl
Of heavy grape? The smoke prevents my seeing
But at brief whiles.—The boarding band has fallen,
Fallen almost to a man.—'Twas well assayed!

MAGENDIE
That's from their "Temeraire," whose vicious broadside
Has cleared poor Lucas' decks.

VILLENEUVE
And Lucas, too.
I see him no more there. His red planks show
Three hundred dead if one. Now for ourselves!

[Four of the English three-deckers have gradually closed round the "Bucentaure," whose bowsprit still sticks fast in the gallery of the "Santisima Trinidad." A broadside comes from one of the English, resulting in worse havoc on the "Bucentaure." The main and mizzen masts of the latter fall, and the boats are beaten to pieces. A raking fire of musketry follows from the attacking ships, to which the "Bucentaure" heroically continues still to keep up a reply.

CAPTAIN MAGENDIE falls wounded. His place is taken by LIEUTENANT DAUDIGNON.]

VILLENEUVE
Now that the fume has lessened, code my biddance
Upon our only mast, and tell the van
At once to wear, and come into the fire.
[Aside] If it be true that, as HE sneers, success
Demands of me but cool audacity,
To-day shall leave him nothing to desire!

[Musketry continues. DAUDIGNON falls. He is removed, his post being taken by LIEUTENANT FOURNIER. Another crash comes, and the deck is suddenly encumbered with rigging.]

FOURNIER
There goes our foremast! How for signalling now?

VILLENEUVE
To try that longer, Fournier, is in vain
Upon this haggard, scorched, and ravaged hulk,
Her decks all reeking with such gory shows,
Her starboard side in rents, her stern nigh gone!
How does she keep afloat?—
"Bucentaure," O lucky good old ship!
My part in you is played. Ay—I must go;
I must tempt Fate elsewhere,—if but a boat
Can bear me through this wreckage to the van.

FOURNIER
Our boats are stove in, or as full of holes
As the cook's skimmer, from their cursed balls!

[Musketry. VILLENEUVE'S Head-of-Staff, DE PRIGNY, falls wounded, and many additional men. VILLENEUVE glances troublously from ship to ship of his fleet.]

VILLENEUVE
How hideous are the waves, so pure this dawn!—
Red-frothed; and friends and foes all mixed therein.—
Can we in some way hail the "Trinidad"
And get a boat from her?

[They attempt to distract the attention of the "Santisima Trinidad" by shouting.]

Impossible;
Amid the loud combustion of this strife
As well try holloing to the antipodes!...
So here I am. The bliss of Nelson's end
Will not be mine; his full refulgent eve
Becomes my midnight! Well; the fleets shall see
That I can yield my cause with dignity.

[The "Bucentaure" strikes her flag. A boat then puts off from the English ship "Conqueror," and
VILLENEUVE, having surrendered his sword, is taken out from the "Bucentaure." But being unable to
regain her own ship, the boat is picked up by the "Mars," and the French admiral is received aboard her.
Point of view changes.]

SCENE IV

THE SAME. THE COCKPIT OF THE "VICTORY"

[A din of trampling and dragging overhead, which is accompanied by a continuos ground-bass roar from
the guns of the warring fleets, culminating at times in loud concussions. The wounded are lying around
in rows for treatment, some groaning, some silently dying, some dead. The gloomy atmosphere of the
low-beamed deck is pervaded by a thick haze of smoke, powdered wood, and other dust, and is heavy
with the fumes of gunpowder and candle-grease, the odour of drugs and cordials, and the smell
from abdominal wounds.

NELSON, his face now pinched and wan with suffering, is lying undressed in a midshipman's berth, dimly
lit by a lantern. DR. BEATTY, DR. MAGRATH, the Rev. DR. SCOTT the Chaplain, BURKE the Purser, the
Steward, and a few others stand around.]

MAGRATH [in a low voice]
Poor Ram, and poor Tom Whipple, have just gone..

BEATTY
There was no hope for them.

NELSON [brokenly]
Who have just died?

BEATTY
Two who were badly hit by now, my lord;
Lieutenant Ram and Mr. Whipple.

NELSON
Ah!
So many lives—in such a glorious cause....
I join them soon, soon, soon!—O where is Hardy?

Will nobody bring Hardy to me—none?
He must be killed, too. Surely Hardy's dead?

A MIDSHIPMAN
He's coming soon, my lord. The constant call
On his full heed of this most mortal fight
Keeps him from hastening hither as he would.

NELSON
I'll wait, I'll wait. I should have thought of it.

[Presently HARDY comes down. NELSON and he grasp hands.]

Hardy, how goes the day with us and England?

HARDY
Well; very well, thank God for't, my dear lord.
Villeneuve their Admiral has this moment struck,
· And put himself aboard the "Conqueror."
Some fourteen of their first-rates, or about,
Thus far we've got. The said "Bucentaure" chief:
The "Santa Ana," the "Redoubtable,"
The "Fougueux," the "Santisima Trinidad,"
"San Augustino, "San Francisco," "Aigle";
And our old "Swiftsure," too, we've grappled back,
To every seaman's joy. But now their van
Has tacked to bear round on the "Victory"
And crush her by sheer weight of wood and brass:
Three of our best I am therefore calling up,
And make no doubt of worsting theirs, and France.

NELSON
That's well. I swore for twenty.—But it's well.

HARDY
We'll have 'em yet! But without you, my lord,
We have to make slow plodding do the deeds
That sprung by inspiration ere you fell;
And on this ship the more particularly.

NELSON
No, Hardy.—Ever 'twas your settled fault
So modestly to whittle down your worth.
But I saw stuff in you which admirals need
When, taking thought, I chose the "Victory's" keel
To do my business with these braggarts in.
A business finished now, for me!—Good friend,
Slow shades are creeping me... I scarce see you.

HARDY
The smoke from ships upon our win'ard side,
And the dust raised by their worm-eaten hulks,
When our balls touch 'em, blind the eyes, in truth.

NELSON
No; it is not that dust; 'tis dust of death
That darkens me.

[A shock overhead. HARDY goes up. On or two other officers go up, and by and by return.]

What was that extra noise?

OFFICER
The "Formidable' passed us by, my lord,
And thumped a stunning broadside into us.—
But, on their side, the "Hero's" captain's fallen;
The "Algeciras" has been boarded, too,
By Captain Tyler, and the captain shot:
Admiral Gravina desperately holds out;
They say he's lost an arm.

NELSON
And we, ourselves—
Who have we lost on board here? Nay, but tell me!

BEATTY
Besides poor Scott, my lord, and Charles Adair,
Lieutenant Ram, and Whipple, captain's clerk,
There's Smith, and Palmer, midshipmen, just killed.
And fifty odd of seamen and marines.

NELSON
Poor youngsters! Scarred old Nelson joins you soon.

BEATTY
And wounded: Bligh, lieutenant; Pasco, too,
and Reeves, and Peake, lieutenants of marines,
And Rivers, Westphall, Bulkeley, midshipmen,
With, of the crew, a hundred odd just now,
Unreckoning those late fallen not brought below.

BURKE
That fellow in the mizzen-top, my lord,
Who made it his affair to wing you thus,
We took good care to settle; and he fell
Like an old rook, smack from his perch, stone dead.

NELSON

'Twas not worth while!—He was, no doubt, a man
Who in simplicity and sheer good faith
Strove but to serve his country. Rest be to him!
And may his wife, his friends, his little ones,
If such be had, be tided through their loss,
And soothed amid the sorrow brought by me.

[HARDY re-enters.]

Who's that? Ah—here you come! How, Hardy, now?

HARDY

The Spanish Admiral's rumoured to be wounded,
We know not with what truth. But, be as 'twill,
He sheers away with all he could call round,
And some few frigates, straight to Cadiz port.

[A violent explosion is heard above the confused noises on deck. A midshipman goes above and returns.]

MIDSHIPMAN [in the background]

It is the enemy's first-rate, the "Achille,"
Blown to a thousand atoms!—While on fire,
Before she burst, the captain's woman there,
Desperate for life, climbed from the gunroom port
Upon the rudder-chains; stripped herself stark,
And swam for the Pickle's boat. Our men in charge,
Seeing her great breasts bulging on the brine,
Sang out, "A mermaid 'tis, by God!"—then rowed
And hauled her in.—

BURKE

Such unbid sights obtrude
On death's dyed stage!

MIDSHIPMAN

Meantime the "Achille" fought on,
Even while the ship was blazing, knowing well
The fire must reach their powder; which it did.
The spot is covered now with floating men,
Some whole, the main in parts; arms, legs, trunks, heads,
Bobbing with tons of timber on the waves,
And splinter looped with entrails of the crew.

NELSON [rousing]

Our course will be to anchor. Let me know.

HARDY
But let me ask, my lord, as needs I must,
Seeing your state, and that our work's not done,
Shall I, from you, bid Admiral Collingwood
Take full on him the conduct of affairs?

NELSON [trying to raise himself]
Not while I live, I hope! No, Hardy; no.
Give Collingwood my order. Anchor all!
HARDY [hesitating]
You mean the signal's to be made forthwith?

NELSON
I do!—By God, if but our carpenter
Could rig me up a jury-backbone now,
To last one hour—until the battle's done,
I'd see to it! But here I am—stove in—
Broken—all logged and done for! Done, ay done!

BEATTY [returning from the other wounded]
My lord, I must implore you to lie calm!
You shorten what at best may not be long.

NELSON [exhausted]
I know, I know, good Beatty! Thank you well
Hardy, I was impatient. Now I am still.
Sit here a moment, if you have time to spare?

[BEATTY and others retire, and the two abide in silence, except for the trampling overhead and the moans from adjoining berths. NELSON is apparently in less pain, seeming to doze.]

NELSON [suddenly]
What are you thinking, that you speak no word?

HARDY [waking from a short reverie]
Thoughts all confused, my lord:—their needs on deck,
Your own sad state, and your unrivalled past;
Mixed up with flashes of old things afar—
Old childish things at home, down Wessex way.
In the snug village under Blackdon Hill
Where I was born. The tumbling stream, the garden,
The placid look of the grey dial there,
Marking unconsciously this bloody hour,
And the red apples on my father's trees,
Just now full ripe.

NELSON
Ay, thus do little things

Steal into my mind, too. But ah, my heart
Knows not your calm philosophy!—There's one—
Come nearer to me, Hardy.—One of all,
As you well guess, pervades my memory now;
She, and my daughter—I speak freely to you.
'Twas good I made that codicil this morning
That you and Blackwood witnessed. Now she rests
Safe on the nation's honour.... Let her have
My hair, and the small treasured things I owned,
And take care of her, as you care for me!

[HARDY promises.]

NELSON [resuming in a murmur]
Does love die with our frame's decease, I wonder,
Or does it live on ever?...

[A silence. BEATTY approaches.]

HARDY
Now I'll leave,
See if your order's gone, and then return.

NELSON [symptoms of death beginning to change his face]
Yes, Hardy; yes; I know it. You must go.—
Here we shall meet no more; since Heaven forfend
That care for me should keep you idle now,
When all the ship demands you. Beatty, too.
Go to the others who lie bleeding there;
Them can you aid. Me you can render none!
My time here is the briefest.—If I live
But long enough I'll anchor.... But—too late—
My anchoring's elsewhere ordered!... Kiss me, Hardy:

[HARDY bends over him.]

I'm satisfied. Thank God, I have done my duty!

[HARDY brushes his eyes with his hand, and withdraws to go above, pausing to look back before he finally disappears.]

BEATTY [watching Nelson]
Ah!—Hush around!...
He's sinking. It is but a trifle now
Of minutes with him. Stand you, please, aside,
And give him air.

[BEATTY, the Chaplain, MAGRATH, the Steward, and attendants continue to regard NELSON. BEATTY looks at his watch.]

BEATTY
Two hours and fifty minutes since he fell,
And now he's going.

[They wait. NELSON dies.]

CHAPLAIN
Yes.... He has homed to where
There's no more sea.

BEATTY
We'll let the Captain know,
Who will confer with Collingwood at once.
I must now turn to these.

[He goes to another part of the cockpit, a midshipman ascends to the deck, and the scene overclouds.]

CHORUS OF THE PITIES [aerial music]
His thread was cut too slowly! When he fell.
And bade his fame farewell,
He might have passed, and shunned his long-drawn pain,
Endured in vain, in vain!

SPIRIT OF THE YEARS
Young Spirits, be not critical of That
Which was before, and shall be after you!

SPIRIT OF THE PITIES
But out of tune the Mode and meritless
That quickens sense in shapes whom, thou hast said,
Necessitation sways! A life there was
Among these self-same frail ones—Sophocles—
Who visioned it too clearly, even while
He dubbed the Will "the gods." Truly said he,
"Such gross injustice to their own creation
Burdens the time with mournfulness for us,
And for themselves with shame." (9)—Things mechanized
By coils and pivots set to foreframed codes
Would, in a thorough-sphered melodic rule,
And governance of sweet consistency,
Be cessed no pain, whose burnings would abide
With That Which holds responsibility,
Or inexist.

SPIRIT OF THE PITIES

Yea, yea, yea!
Thus would the Mover pay
The score each puppet owes,
The Reaper reap what his contrivance sows!
Why make Life debtor when it did not buy?
Why wound so keenly Right that it would die?

SPIRIT OF THE YEARS
Nay, blame not! For what judgment can ye blame?—
In that immense unweeting Mind is shown
One far above forethinking; processive,
Yet superconscious; a Clairvoyancy
That knows not what It knows, yet works therewith.—
The cognizance ye mourn, Life's doom to feel,
If I report it meetly, came unmeant,
Emerging with blind gropes from impercipience
By listless sequence—luckless, tragic Chance,
In your more human tongue.

SPIRIT OF THE PITIES
And hence unneeded
In the economy of Vitality,
Which might have ever kept a sealed cognition
As doth the Will Itself.

CHORUS OF THE YEARS [aerial music]
Nay, nay, nay;
Your hasty judgments stay,
Until the topmost cyme
Have crowned the last entablature of Time.
O heap not blame on that in-brooding Will;
O pause, till all things all their days fulfil!

SCENE V

LONDON. THE GUILDHALL

[A crowd of citizens has gathered outside to watch the carriages as they drive up and deposit guests invited to the Lord Mayor's banquet, for which event the hall is brilliantly lit within. A cheer rises when the equipage of any popular personage arrives at the door.

FIRST CITIZEN
Well, well! Nelson is the man who ought to have been banqueted to-night. But he is coming to Town in a coach different from these.!

SECOND CITIZEN

Will they bring his poor splintered body home?

FIRST CITIZEN
Yes. They say he's to be tombed in marble, at St. Paul's or Westminster. We shall see him if he lays in state. It will make a patriotic spectacle for a fine day.

BOY
How can you see a dead man, father, after so long?

FIRST CITIZEN
They'll embalm him, my boy, as they did all the great Egyptian admirals.

BOY
His lady will be handy for that, won't she?

FIRST CITIZEN
Don't ye ask awkward questions.

SECOND CITIZEN
Here's another coming!

FIRST CITIZEN
That's my Lord Chancellor Eldon. Wot he'll say, and wot he'll look!
Mr. Pitt will be here soon.

BOY
I don't like Billy. He killed Uncle John's parrot.

SECOND CITIZEN
How may ye make that out, youngster?

BOY
Mr. Pitt made the war, and the war made us want sailors; and Uncle John went for a walk down Wapping High Street to talk to the pretty ladies one evening; and there was a press all along the river that night—a regular hot one—and Uncle John was carried on board a man-of-war to fight under Nelson; and nobody minded Uncle John's parrot, and it talked itself to death. So Mr. Pitt killed Uncle John's parrot; see it, sir?

SECOND CITIZEN
You had better have a care of this boy, friend. His brain is too precious for the common risks of Cheapside. Not but what he might as well have said Boney killed the parrot when he was about it. And as for Nelson—who's now sailing shinier seas than ours, if they've rubbed Her off his slate where he's gone to,—the French papers say that our loss in him is greater than our gain in ships; so that logically the victory is theirs. Gad, sir, it's almost true!

[A hurrahing is heard from Cheapside, and the crowd in that direction begins to hustle and show excitement.]

FIRST CITIZEN
He's coming, he's coming! Here, let me lift you up, my boy.— Why, they have taken out the horses, as I am man alive!

SECOND CITIZEN
Pitt for ever!—Why, here's a blade opening and shutting his mouth like the rest, but never a sound does he raise!

THIRD CITIZEN
I've not too much breath to carry me through my day's work, so I can't afford to waste it in such luxuries as crying Hurrah to aristocrats. If ye was ten yards off y'd think I was shouting as loud as any.

SECOND CITIZEN
It's a very mean practice of ye to husband yourself at such a time, and gape in dumbshow like a frog in Plaistow Marshes.

THIRD CITIZEN
No, sir; it's economy; a very necessary instinct in these days of ghastly taxations to pay half the armies in Europe! In short, in the word of the Ancients, it is scarcely compass-mentas to do otherwise! Somebody must save something, or the country will be as bankrupt as Mr. Pitt himself is, by all account; though he don't look it just now.

[PITT's coach passes, drawn by a troop of running men and boy. The Prime Minister is seen within, a thin, erect, up-nosed figure, with a flush of excitement on his usually pale face. The vehicle reached the doorway to the Guildhall and halts with a jolt. PITT gets out shakily, and amid cheers enters the building.]

FOURTH CITIZEN
Quite a triumphal entry. Such is power;
Now worshipped, now accursed! The overthrow
Of all Pitt's European policy
When his hired army and his chosen general
Surrendered them at Ulm a month ago,
Is now forgotten! Ay; this Trafalgar
Will botch up many a ragged old repute,
Make Nelson figure as domestic saint
No less than country's saviour, Pitt exalt
As zenith-star of England's firmament,
And uncurse all the bogglers of her weal
At this adventurous time.

THIRD CITIZEN
Talk of Pitt being ill. He looks hearty as a buck.

FIRST CITIZEN
It's the news—no more. His spirits are up like a rocket for the moment.

BOY

Is it because Trafalgar is near Portugal that he loves Port wine?

SECOND CITIZEN
Ah, as I said, friend; this boy must go home and be carefully put to bed!

FIRST CITIZEN
Well, whatever William's faults, it is a triumph for his virtues to-night!

[PITT having disappeared, the Guildhall doors are closed, and the crowd slowly disperses, till in the course of an hour the street shows itself empty and dark, only a few oil lamps burning.

The SCENE OPENS, revealing the interior of the Guildhall, and the brilliant assembly of City magnates, Lords, and Ministers seated there, Mr. PITT occupying a chair of honour by the Lord Mayor. His health has been proposed as that of the Saviour of England, and drunk with acclamations.]

PITT [standing up after repeated calls]
My lords and gentlemen:—You have toasted me
As one who has saved England and her cause.
I thank you, gentlemen, unfeignedly.
But—no man has saved England, let me say:
England has saved herself, by her exertions:
She will, I trust, save Europe by her example!

[Loud applause, during which he sits down, rises, and sits down again. The scene then shuts, and the night without has place.]

SPIRIT OF THE YEARS
Those words of this man Pitt—his last large words,
As I may prophesy—that ring to-night
In their first mintage to the feasters here,
Will spread with ageing, lodge, and crystallize,
And stand embedded in the English tongue
Till it grow thin, outworn, and cease to be.—
So is't ordained by That Which all ordains;
For words were never winged with apter grace.
Or blent with happier choice of time and place,
To hold the imagination of this strenuous race.

SCENE VI (10)

AN INN AT RENNES

[Night. A sleeping-chamber. Two candles are burning near a bed in an alcove, and writing-materials are on the table.

The French admiral, VILLENEUVE, partly undressed, is pacing up and down the room.]

VILLENEUVE
These hauntings have at last nigh proved to me
That this thing must be done. Illustrious foe
And teacher, Nelson: blest and over blest
In thy outgoing at the noon of strife
When glory clasped thee round; while wayward Death
Refused my coaxings for the like-timed call!
Yet I did press where thickest missiles fell,
And both by precept and example showed
Where lay the line of duty, patriotism,
And honour, in that combat of despair.

[He see himself in the glass as he passes.]

Unfortunate Villeneuve!—whom fate has marked
To suffer for too firm a faithfulness.—
An Emperor's chide is a command to die.—
By him accursed, forsaken by my friend,
Awhile stern England's prisoner, then unloosed
Like some poor dolt unworth captivity,
Time serves me now for ceasing. Why not cease?...
When, as Shades whisper in the chasmal night,
"Better, far better, no percipience here."—
O happy lack, that I should have no child
To come into my hideous heritage,
And groan beneath the burden of my name! (11)

SPIRIT OF THE YEARS
I'll speak. His mood is ripe for such a parle.

[Sending a voice into VILLENEUVE'S ear.]

Thou dost divine the hour!

VILLENEUVE
But those stern Nays,
That heretofore were audible to me
At each unhappy time I strove to pass?

SPIRIT OF THE YEARS
Have been annulled. The Will grants exit freely;
Yea, It says "Now." Therefore make now thy time.

SPIRIT OF THE PITIES
May his sad sunken soul merge into nought
Meekly and gently as a breeze at eve!

VILLENEUVE
From skies above me and the air around
Those callings which so long have circled me
At last do whisper "Now." Now it shall be!

[He seals a letter, and addresses it to his wife; then takes a dagger from his accoutrements that are hanging alongside, and, lying down upon his back on the bed, stabs himself determinedly in many places, leaving the weapon in the last wound.]

Ungrateful master; generous foes; Farewell!

[VILLENEUVE dies; and the scene darkens.]

SCENE VII

KING GEORGE'S WATERING-PLACE, SOUTH WESSEX

[The interior of the "Old Rooms" Inn. Boatmen and burghers are sitting on settles round the fire, smoking and drinking.

FIRST BURGHER
So they've brought him home at last, hey? And he's to be solemnized with a roaring funeral?

FIRST BOATMAN
Yes, thank God.... 'Tis better to lie dry than wet, if canst do it without stinking on the road gravewards. And they took care that he shouldn't.

SECOND BOATMAN
'Tis to be at Paul's; so they say that know. And the crew of the "Victory" have to walk in front, and Captain Hardy is to carry his stars and garters on a great velvet pincushion.

FIRST BURGHER
Where's the Captain now?

SECOND BOATMAN [nodding in the direction of Captain Hardy's house]
Down at home here biding with his own folk a bit. I zid en walking with them on the Esplanade yesterday. He looks ten years older than he did when he went. Ay—he brought the galliant hero home!

SECOND BURGHER
Now how did they bring him home so that he could lie in state afterwards to the naked eye!

FIRST BOATMAN
Well, as they always do,—in a cask of sperrits.

SECOND BURGHER
Really, now!

FIRST BOATMAN [lowering his voice]
But what happened was this. They were a long time coming, owing to contrary winds, and the "Victory" being little more than a wreck. And grog ran short, because they'd used near all they had to peckle his body in. So—they broached the Adm'l!

SECOND BURGHER
How?

FIRST BOATMAN
Well; the plain calendar of it is, that when he came to be unhooped, it was found that the crew had drunk him dry. What was the men to do? Broke down by the battle, and hardly able to keep afloat, 'twas a most defendable thing, and it fairly saved their lives. So he was their salvation after death as he had been in the fight. If he could have knowed it, 'twould have pleased him down to the ground! How 'a would have laughed through the spigot-hole: "Draw on, my hearties! Better I shrivel that you famish." Ha-ha!

SECOND BURGHER
It may be defendable afloat; but it seems queer ashore.

FIRST BOATMAN
Well, that's as I had it from one that knows—Bob Loveday of Overcombe—one of the "Victory" men that's going to walk in the funeral. However, let's touch a livelier string. Peter Green, strike up that new ballet that they've lately had prented here, and were hawking about town last market-day.

SONG

THE NIGHT OF TRAFALGAR
I
In the wild October night-time, when the wind raved round the land,
And the Back-sea (12) met the Front-sea, and our doors were blocked with sand,
And we heard the drub of Dead-man's Bay, where bones of thousands are,
We knew not what the day had done for us at Trafalgar.
[All] Had done,
Had done,
For us at Trafalgar!

II
"Pull hard, and make the Nothe, or down we go!" one says, says he.
We pulled; and bedtime brought the storm; but snug at home slept we.
Yet all the while our gallants after fighting through the day,
Were beating up and down the dark, sou'-west of Cadiz Bay.
The dark,
The dark,
Sou'-west of Cadiz Bay!

III
The victors and the vanquished then the storm it tossed and tore,

As hard they strove, those worn-out men, upon that surly shore;
Dead Nelson and his half-dead crew, his foes from near and far,
Were rolled together on the deep that night at Trafalgar!
The deep,
The deep,
That night at Trafalgar!

[The Cloud-curtain draws.]

CHORUS OF THE YEARS
Meanwhile the month moves on to counter-deeds
Vast as the vainest needs,
And fiercely the predestined plot proceeds.

ACT SIXTH

SCENE I

THE FIELD OF AUSTERLITZ. THE FRENCH POSITION

[The night is the 1st of December following, and the eve of the battle. The view is from the elevated
position of the Emperor's bivouac. The air cuts keen and the sky glistens with stars, but the lower levels
are covered with a white fog stretching like a sea, from which the heights protrude as dusky rocks.

To the left are discernible high and wooded hills. In the front mid-distance the plateau of Pratzen
outstands, declining suddenly on the right to a low flat country covered with marshes and pools now
mostly obscured. On the plateau itself are seen innumerable and varying lights, marking the bivouac of
the centre divisions of the Austro-Russian army. Close to the foreground the fires of the French are
burning, surrounded by soldiery. The invisible presence of the countless thousand of massed humanity
that compose the two armies makes itself felt indefinably.

The tent of NAPOLEON rises nearest at hand, with sentinel and other military figures looming around,
and saddled horses held by attendants. The accents of the Emperor are audible, through the canvas
from inside, dictating a proclamation.]

VOICE OF NAPOLEON
"Soldiers, the hordes of Muscovy now face you,
To mend the Austrian overthrow at Ulm!
But how so? Are not these the self-same bands
You met and swept aside at Hollabrunn,
And whose retreating forms, dismayed to flight,
Your feet pursued along the trackways here?

"Our own position, massed and menacing,
Is rich in chance for opportune attack;

For, say they march to cross and turn our right—
A course almost at their need—their stretching flank
Will offer us, from points now prearranged—-"

VOICE OF A MARSHAL
Shows it, your Majesty, the wariness
That marks your usual far-eye policy,
To openly announce your tactics thus
Some twelve hours ere their form can actualize?

THE VOICE OF NAPOLEON
The zest such knowledge will impart to all
Is worth the risk of leakages. [To Secretary]
Write on.

[Dictation resumed]

"Soldiers, your sections I myself shall lead;
But ease your minds who would expostulate
Against my undue rashness. If your zeal
Sow hot confusion in the hostile files
As your old manner is, and in our rush
We mingle with our foes, I'll use fit care.
Nevertheless, should issues stand at pause
But for a wink-while, that time you will eye
Your Emperor the foremost in the shock,
Taking his risk with every ranksman here.
For victory, men, must be no thing surmised,
As that which may or may not beam on us,
Like noontide sunshine on a dubious morn;
It must be sure!—The honour and the fame
Of France's gay and gallant infantry—
So dear, so cherished all the Empire through—
Binds us to compass it!
Maintain the ranks;
Let none be thinned by impulse or excuse
Of bearing back the wounded: and, in fine,
Be every one in this conviction firm:—
That 'tis our sacred bond to overthrow
These hirelings of a country not their own:
Yea, England's hirelings, they!—a realm stiff-steeled
In deathless hatred of our land and lives.

"The campaign closes with this victory;
And we return to find our standards joined
By vast young armies forming now in France.
Forthwith resistless, Peace establish we,
Worthy of you, the nation, and of me!"

"NAPOLEON."
[To his Marshals]
So shall we prostrate these paid slaves of hers—
England's, I mean—the root of all the war.

VOICE OF MURAT
The further details sent of Trafalgar
Are not assuring.

VOICE OF LANNES
What may the details be?

VOICE OF NAPOLEON [moodily]
We learn that six-and-twenty ships of war,
During the fight and after, struck their flags,
And that the tigerish gale throughout the night
Gave fearful finish to the English rage.
By luck their Nelson's gone, but gone withal
Are twenty thousand prisoners, taken off
To gnaw their finger-nails in British hulks.
Of our vast squadrons of the summer-time
But rags and splintered remnants now remain.—
Thuswise Villeneuve, poor craven, quitted him!
And England puffed to yet more bombastry.
—Well, well; I can't be everywhere. No matter;
A victory's brewing here as counterpoise!
These water-rats may paddle in their salt slush,
And welcome. 'Tis not long they'll have the lead.
Ships can be wrecked by land!

ANOTHER VOICE
And how by land,
Your Majesty, if one may query such?

VOICE OF NAPOLEON [sardonically]
I'll bid all states of Europe shut their ports
To England's arrogant bottoms, slowly starve
Her bloated revenues and monstrous trade,
Till all her hulls lie sodden in their docks,
And her grey island eyes in vain shall seek
One jack of hers upon the ocean plains!

VOICE OF SOULT
A few more master-strokes, your Majesty,
Must be dealt hereabout to compass such!

VOICE OF NAPOLEON
God, yes!—Even here Pitt's guineas are the foes:

'Tis all a duel 'twixt this Pitt and me;
And, more than Russia's host, and Austria's flower,
I everywhere to-night around me feel
As from an unseen monster haunting nigh
His country's hostile breath!—But come: to choke it
By our to-morrow's feats, which now, in brief,
I recapitulate.—First Soult will move
To forward the grand project of the day:
Namely: ascend in echelon, right to front,
With Vandamme's men, and those of Saint Hilaire:
Legrand's division somewhere further back—
Nearly whereat I place my finger here—
To be there reinforced by tirailleurs:
Lannes to the left here, on the Olmutz road,
Supported by Murat's whole cavalry.
While in reserve, here, are the grenadiers
Of Oudinot, the corps of Bernadotte,
Rivaud, Drouet, and the Imperial Guard.

MARSHAL'S VOICES
Even as we understood, Sire, and have ordered.
Nought lags but day, to light our victory!

VOICE OF NAPOLEON
Now let us up and ride the bivouacs round,
And note positions ere the soldiers sleep.
—Omit not from to-morrow's home dispatch
Direction that this blow of Trafalgar
Be hushed in all the news-sheets sold in France,
Or, if reported, let it be portrayed
As a rash fight whereout we came not worst,
But were so broken by the boisterous eve
That England claims to be the conqueror.

[There emerge from the tent NAPOLEON and the marshals, who all mount the horses that are led up, and proceed through the frost and time towards the bivouacs. At the Emperor's approach to the nearest soldiery they spring up.]

SOLDIERS
The Emperor! He's here! The Emperor's here!

AN OLD GRENADIER [approaching Napoleon familiarly]
We'll bring thee Russian guns and flags galore.
To celebrate thy coronation-day!

[They gather into wisps the straw, hay, and other litter on which they have been lying, and kindling these at the dying fires, wave them as torches. This is repeated as each fire is reached, till the whole

French position is one wide illumination. The most enthusiastic of the soldiers follow the Emperor in a throng as he progresses, and his whereabouts in the vast field is denoted by their cries.]

CHORUS OF PITIES [aerial music]
Strange suasive pull of personality!

CHORUS OF IRONIC SPIRITS
His projects they unknow, his grin unsee!

CHORUS OF THE PITIES
Their luckless hearts say blindly—He!

[The night-shades close over.]

SCENE II

THE SAME. THE RUSSIAN POSITION

[Midnight at the quarters of FIELD-MARSHAL PRINCE KUTUZOF at Kresnowitz. An inner apartment is discovered, roughly adapted as a council-room. On a table with candles is unfolded a large map of Austerlitz and its environs.

The Generals are assembled in consultation round the table, WEIROTHER pointing to the map, LANGERON, BUXHOVDEN, and MILORADOVICH standing by, DOKHTOROF bending over the map, PRSCHEBISZEWSKY (13) indifferently walking up and down. KUTUZOF, old and weary, with a scarred face and only one eye, is seated in a chair at the head of the table, nodding, waking, and nodding again. Some officers of lower grade are in the background, and horses in waiting are heard hoofing and champing outside.

WEIROTHER speaks, referring to memoranda, snuffing the nearest candle, and moving it from place to place on the map as he proceeds importantly.]

WEIROTHER
Now here, our right, along the Olmutz Road
Will march and oust our counterfacers there,
Dislodge them from the Sainton Hill, and thence
Advance direct to Brunn.—You heed me, sirs?—
The cavalry will occupy the plain:
Our centre and main strength,—you follow me?—
Count Langeron, Dokhtorof, with Prschebiszewsky
And Kollowrath—now on the Pratzen heights—
Will down and cross the Goldbach rivulet,
Seize Tilnitz, Kobelnitz, and hamlets nigh,
Turn the French right, move onward in their rear,
Cross Schwarsa, hold the great Vienna road:—
So, with the nightfall, centre, right, and left,

Will rendezvous beneath the walls of Brunn.

LANGERON [taking a pinch of snuff]
Good, General; very good!—if Bonaparte
Will kindly stand and let you have your way.
But what if he do not!—if he forestall
These sound slow movements, mount the Pratzen hills
When we descend, fall on OUR rear forthwith,
While we go crying for HIS rear in vain?

KUTUZOF [waking up]
Ay, ay, Weirother; that's the question—eh?

WEIROTHER [impatiently]
If Bonaparte had meant to climb up there,
Being one so spry and so determinate,
He would have set about it ere this eve!
He has not troops to do so, sirs, I say:
His utmost strength is forty thousand men.

LANGERON
Then if so weak, how can so wise a brain
Court ruin by abiding calmly here
The impact of a force so large as ours?
He may be mounting up this very hour!
What think you, General Miloradovich?

MILORADOVICH
I? What's the use of thinking, when to-morrow
Will tell us, with no need to think at all!

WEIROTHER
Pah! At this moment he retires apace.
His fires are dark; all sounds have ceased that way
Save voice of owl or mongrel wintering there.
But, were he nigh, these movements I detail
Would knock the bottom from his enterprize.

KUTUZOF [rising]
Well, well. Now this being ordered, set it going.
One here shall make fair copies of the notes,
And send them round. Colonel van Toll I ask
To translate part.—Generals, it grows full late,
And half-a-dozen hours of needed sleep
Will aid us more than maps. We now disperse,
And luck attend us all. Good-night. Good-night.

[The Generals and other officers go out severally.]

Such plans are—paper! Only to-morrow's light
Reveals the true manoeuvre to my sight!

[He flaps out with his hand all the candles but one or two, slowly walks outside the house, and listens. On the high ground in the direction of the French lines are heard shouts, and a wide illumination grows and strengthens; but the hollows are still mantled in fog.]

Are these the signs of regiments out of heart,
And beating backward from an enemy!

[He remains pondering. On the Pratzen heights immediately in front there begins a movement among the Russians, signifying that the plan which involves desertion of that vantage-ground is about to be put in force. Noises of drunken singing arise from the Russian lines at various points elsewhere.

The night shades involve the whole.]

SCENE III

THE SAME. THE FRENCH POSITION

[Shortly before dawn on the morning of the 2nd of December. A white frost and fog still prevail in the low-lying areas; but overhead the sky is clear. A dead silence reigns.

NAPOLEON, on a grey horse, closely attended by BERTHIER, and surrounded by MARSHALS SOULT, LANNES, MURAT, and their aides-de camp, all cloaked, is discernible in the gloom riding down from the high ground before Bellowitz, on which they have bivouacked, to the village of Puntowitz on the Goldbach stream, quite near the front of the Russian position of the day before on the Pratzen crest. The Emperor and his companions come to a pause, look around and upward to the hills, and listen.]

NAPOLEON
Their bivouac fires, that lit the top last night,
Are all extinct.

LANNES
And hark you, Sire; I catch
A sound which, if I err not, means the thing
We have hoped, and hoping, feared fate would not yield!

NAPOLEON
My God, it surely is the tramp of horse
And jolt of cannon downward from the hill
Toward our right here, by the swampy lakes
That face Davout? Thus, as I sketched, they work!

MURAT

Yes! They already move upon Tilnitz.

NAPOLEON
Leave them alone! Nor stick nor stone we'll stir
To interrupt them. Nought that we can scheme
Will help us like their own stark sightlessness!—
Let them get down to those white lowlands there,
And so far plunge in the level that no skill,
When sudden vision flashes on their fault,
Can help them, though despair-stung, to regain
The key to mastery held at yestereve!

Meantime move onward these divisions here
Under the fog's kind shroud; descend the slope,
And cross the stream below the Russian lines:
There halt concealed, till I send down the word.

[NAPOLEON and his staff retire to the hill south-east of Bellowitz and the day dawns pallidly.]

'Tis good to get above that rimy cloak
And into cleaner air. It chilled me through.

[When they reach the summit they are over the fog: and suddenly the sun breaks forth to the left of Pratzen, illuminating the ash-hued face of NAPOLEON and the faces of those around him. All eyes are turned first to the sun, and thence to look for the dense masses of men that had occupied the upland the night before.]

MURAT
I see them not. The plateau seems deserted!

NAPOLEON
Gone; verily!—Ah, how much will you bid,
An hour hence, for the coign abandoned now!
The battle's ours.—It was, then, their rash march
Downwards to Tilnitz and the Goldbach swamps
Before dawn, that we heard.—No hurry, Lannes!
Enjoy this sun, that rests its chubby jowl
Upon the plain, and thrusts its bristling beard
Across the lowlands' fleecy counterpane,
Peering beneath our broadest hat-brims' shade....
Soult, how long hence to win the Pratzen top?

SOULT
Some twenty minutes or less, your Majesty:
Our troops down there, still mantled by the mist,
Are half upon the way.

NAPOLEON

Good! Set forthwith
Vandamme and Saint Hilaire to mount the slopes—-

[Firing begins in the marsh to the right by Tilnitz and the pools, though the thick air yet hides the operations.]

O, there you are, blind boozy Buxhovden!
Achieve your worst. Davout will hold you firm.

[The head of and aide-de-camp rises through the fog on that side, and he hastens up to NAPOLEON and his companions, to whom the officer announces what has happened. DAVOUT rides off, disappearing legs first into the white stratum that covers the attack.]

Lannes and Murat, you have concern enough
Here on the left, with Prince Bagration
And all the Austro-Russian cavalry.
Haste off. The victory promising to-day
Will, like a thunder-clap, conclude the war!

[The Marshals with their aides gallop away towards their respective divisions. Soon the two divisions under SOULT are seen ascending in close column the inclines of the Pratzen height. Thereupon the heads of the Russian centre columns disclose themselves, breaking the sky-line of the summit from the other side, in a desperate attempt to regain the position vacated by the Russian left. A fierce struggle develops there between SOULT'S divisions and these, who, despite their tardy attempt to recover the lost post of dominance, are pressed by the French off the slopes into the lowland.]

SEMICHORUS I OF THE PITIES [aerial music]
O Great Necessitator, heed us now!
If it indeed must be
That this day Austria smoke with slaughtery,
Quicken the issue as Thou knowest how;
And dull their lodgment in a flesh that galls!

SEMICHORUS II
If it be in the future human story
To lift this man to yet intenser glory,
Let the exploit be done
With the least sting, or none,
To those, his kind, at whose expense such pitch is won!

SPIRIT OF THE YEARS
Again ye deprecate the World-Soul's way
That I so long have told? Then note anew
[Since ye forget] the ordered potencies,
Nerves, sinews, trajects, eddies, ducts of It
The Eternal Urger, pressing change on change.

[At once, as earlier, a preternatural clearness possesses the atmosphere of the battle-field, in which the scene becomes anatomized and the living masses of humanity transparent. The controlling Immanent Will appears therein, as a brain-like network of currents and ejections, twitching, interpenetrating, entangling, and thrusting hither and thither the human forms.]

SEMICHORUS I OF IRONIC SPIRITS [aerial music]
O Innocents, can ye forget
That things to be were shaped and set
Ere mortals and this planet met?

SEMICHORUS II
Stand ye apostrophizing That
Which, working all, works but thereat
Like some sublime fermenting-vat.

SEMICHORUS I
Heaving throughout its vast content
With strenuously transmutive bent
Though of its aim insentient?—

SEMICHORUS II
Could ye have seen Its early deeds
Ye would not cry, as one who pleads
For quarter, when a Europe bleeds!

SEMICHORUS I
Ere ye, young Pities, had upgrown
From out the deeps where mortals moan
Against a ruling not their own,

SEMICHORUS II
He of the Years beheld, and we,
Creation's prentice artistry
Express in forms that now unbe

SEMICHORUS I
Tentative dreams from day to day;
Mangle its types, re-knead the clay
In some more palpitating way;

SEMICHORUS II
Beheld the rarest wrecked amain,
Whole nigh-perfected species slain
By those that scarce could boast a brain;

SEMICHORUS I
Saw ravage, growth, diminish, add,
Here peoples sane, there peoples mad,

In choiceless throws of good and bad;

SEMICHORUS II
Heard laughters at the ruthless dooms
Which tortured to the eternal glooms
Quick, quivering hearts in hecatombs.

CHORUS
Us Ancients, then, it ill befits
To quake when Slaughter's spectre flits
Athwart this field of Austerlitz!

SHADE OF THE EARTH
Pain not their young compassions by such lore,
But hold you mute, and read the battle yonder:
The moment marks the day's catastrophe.

SCENE IV

THE SAME. THE RUSSIAN POSITION

[It is about noon, and the vital spectacle is now near the village of Tilnitz. The fog has dispersed, and the sun shines clearly, though without warmth, the ice on the pools gleaming under its radiance.

GENERAL BUXHOVDEN and his aides-de-camp have reined up, and remain at pause on a hillock. The General watches through a glass his battalions, which are still disputing the village. Suddenly approach down the track from the upland of Pratzen large companies of Russian infantry helter-skelter. COUNT LANGERON is beheld to be retreating with them; and soon, pale and agitated, he hastens up to GENERAL BUXHOVDEN, whose face is flushed.]

LANGERON
While they are upon us you stay idle here!
Prschebiszewsky's column is distraught and rent,
And more than half my own made captive! Yea,
Kreznowitz carried, and Sokolnitz hemmed:
The enemy's whole strength will stound you soon!

BUXHOVDEN
You seem to see the enemy everywhere.

LANGERON
You cannot see them, be they here or no!

BUXHOVDEN
I only wait Prschebiszewsky's nearing corps
To join Dokhtorof's to them. Here they come.

[SOULT, supported by BERNADOTTE and OUDINOT, having cleared and secured the Pratzen height, his battalions are perceived descending from it on this side, behind DOKHTOROF'S division, so placing the latter between themselves and the pools.]

LANGERON
You cannot tell the Frenchmen from ourselves!
These are the victors.—Ah—Dokhtorof—lost!

[DOKHTOROF'S troops are seen to be retreating towards the water. The watchers stand in painful tenseness.]

BUXHOVDEN
Dokhtorof tell to save him as he may!
We, Count, must gather up our shaken flesh
And hurry them by the road through Austerlitz.

[BUXHOVDEN'S regiments and the remains of LANGERON'S are rallied and collected, and they retreat by way of the hamlet of Aujezd. As they go over the summit of a hill BUXHOVDEN looks back. LANGERON'S columns, which were behind his own, have been cut off by VANDAMME'S division coming down from the Pratzen plateau. This and some detachments from DOKHTOROF'S column rush towards the Satschan lake and endeavour to cross it on the ice. It cracks beneath their weight. At the same moment NAPOLEON and his brilliant staff appear on the top of the Pratzen.

The Emperor watches the scene with a vulpine smile; and directs a battery near at hand to fire down upon the ice on which the Russians are crossing. A ghastly crash and splashing follows the discharge, the shining surface breaking into pieces like a mirror, which fly in all directions. Two thousand fugitives are engulfed, and their groans of despair reach the ears of the watchers like ironical huzzas.

A general flight of the Russian army from wing to wing is now disclosed, involving in its current the EMPEROR ALEXANDER and the EMPEROR FRANCIS, with the reserve, who are seen towards Austerlitz endeavouring to rally their troops in vain. They are swept along by the disordered soldiery.]

SCENE V

THE SAME. NEAR THE WINDMILL OF PALENY

[The mill is about seven miles to the southward, between French advanced posts and the Austrians.

A bivouac fire is burning. NAPOLEON, in grey overcoat and beaver hat turned up front to back, rides to the spot with BERTHIER, SAVARY, and his aides, and alights. He walks to and fro complacently, meditating or talking to BERTHIER. Two groups of officers, one from each army, stand in the background on their respective sides.]

NAPOLEON
What's this of Alexander? Weep, did he,

Like his old namesake, but for meaner cause?
Ha, ha!

BERTHIER
Word goes, you Majesty, that Colonel Toll,
One of Field-Marshal Price Kutuzof's staff,
In the retreating swirl of overthrow,
Found Alexander seated on a stone,
Beneath a leafless roadside apple-tree,
Out here by Goding on the Holitsch way;
His coal-black uniform and snowy plume
Unmarked, his face disconsolate, his grey eyes
Mourning in tears the fate of his brave array—
All flying southward, save the steadfast slain.

NAPOLEON
Poor devil!—But he'll soon get over it—
Sooner than his employers oversea!—
Ha!—this well make friend Pitt and England writhe,
And cloud somewhat their lustrous Trafalgar.

[An open carriage approaches from the direction of Holitsch, accompanied by a small escort of
Hungarian guards. NAPOLEON walks forward to meet it as it draws up, and welcomes the Austrian
Emperor, who alights. He is wearing a grey cloak over a white uniform, carries a light walking-cane, and
is attended by PRINCE JOHN OF LICHTENSTEIN, SWARZENBERG, and others. His fresh-coloured face
contrasts strangely with the bluish pallor of NAPOLEON'S; but it is now thin and anxious.

They formally embrace. BERTHIER, PRINCE JOHN, and the rest retire, and the two Emperors are left by
themselves before the fire.]

NAPOLEON
Here on the roofless ground do I receive you—
My only mansion for these two months past!

FRANCIS
Your tenancy thereof has brought such fame
That it must needs be one which charms you, Sire.

NAPOLEON
Good! Now this war. It has been forced on me
Just at a crisis most inopportune,
When all my energies and arms were bent
On teaching England that her watery walls
Are no defence against the wrath of France
Aroused by breach of solemn covenants.

FRANCIS
I had no zeal for violating peace

Till ominous events in Italy
Revealed the gloomy truth that France aspires
To conquest there, and undue sovereignty.
Since when mine eyes have seen no sign outheld
To signify a change of purposings.

NAPOLEON
Yet there were terms distinctly specified
To General Giulay in November past,
Whereon I'd gladly fling the sword aside.
To wit: that hot armigerent jealousy
Stir us no further on transalpine rule,
I'd take the Isonzo River as our bounds.

FRANCIS
Roundly, that I cede all!—And how may stand
Your views as to the Russian forces here?

NAPOLEON
You have all to lose by that alliance, Sire.
Leave Russia. Let the Emperor Alexander
Make his own terms; whereof the first must be
That he retire from Austrian territory.
I'll grant an armistice therefor. Anon
I'll treat with him to weld a lasting peace,
Based on some simple undertakings; chief,
That Russian armies keep to the ports of his domain.
Meanwhile to you I'll tender this good word:
Keep Austria to herself. To Russia bound,
You pay your own costs with your provinces,
Alexander's likewise therewithal.

FRANCIS
I see as much, and long have seen it, Sire;
And standing here the vanquished, let me own
What happier issues might have left unsaid:
Long, long I have lost the wish to bind myself
To Russia's purposings and Russia's risks;
Little do I count these alliances
With Powers that have no substance seizable!

[As they converse they walk away.]

AN AUSTRIAN OFFICER
O strangest scene of an eventful life,
This junction that I witness here to-day!
An Emperor—in whose majestic veins
Aeneas and the proud Caesarian line

Claim yet to live; and, those scarce less renowned,
The dauntless Hawks'-Hold Counts, of gallantry
So great in fame one thousand years ago—
To bend with deference and manners mild
In talk with this adventuring campaigner,
Raised but by pikes above the common herd!

ANOTHER AUSTRIAN OFFICER
Ay! There be Satschan swamps and Pratzen heights
In royal lines, as here at Austerlitz.

[The Emperors again draw near.]

FRANCIS
Then, to this armistice, which shall be called
Immediately at all points, I agree;
And pledge my word that my august ally
Accept it likewise, and withdraw his force
By daily measured march to his own realm.

NAPOLEON
For him I take your word. And pray believe
That rank ambitions are your own, not mine;
That though I have postured as your enemy,
And likewise Alexander's, we are one
In interests, have in all things common cause.

One country sows these mischiefs Europe through
By her insidious chink of luring ore—
False-featured England, who, to aggrandize
Her name, her influence, and her revenues,
Schemes to impropriate the whole world's trade,
And starves and bleeds the folk of other lands.
Her rock-rimmed situation walls her off
Like a slim selfish mollusk in its shell
From the wide views and fair fraternities
Which on the mainland we reciprocate,
And quicks her quest for profit in our woes!

FRANCIS
I am not competent, your Majesty,
To estimate that country's conscience now,
Nor engage on my ally's behalf
That English ships be shut from Russian trade.
But joyful am I that in all things else
My promise can be made; and that this day
Our conference ends in friendship and esteem.

NAPOLEON
I will send Savary at to-morrow's blink
And make all lucid to the Emperor.
For us, I wholly can avow as mine
The cordial spirit of your Majesty.

[They retire towards the carriage of FRANCIS. BERTHIER, SAVARY, LICHTENSTEIN, and the suite of
officers advance from the background, and with mutual gestures of courtesy and amicable leave-takings
the two Emperors part company.]

CHORUS OF THE PITIES [aerial music]
Each for himself, his family, his heirs;
For the wan weltering nations who concerns, who cares?

CHORUS OF IRONIC SPIRITS
A pertinent query, in truth!—
But spoil not the sport by your ruth:
'Tis enough to make half
Yonder zodiac laugh
When rulers begin to allude
To their lack of ambition,
And strong opposition
To all but the general good!
SPIRIT OF THE YEARS

Hush levities. Events press: turn ye westward.

[A nebulous curtain draws slowly across.]

SCENE VI

SHOCKERWICK HOUSE, NEAR BATH

[The interior of the Picture Gallery. Enter WILTSHIRE, the owner, and Pitt, who looks emaciated and
walks feebly.]

WILTSHIRE [pointing to a portrait]
Now here you have the lady we discussed:
A fine example of his manner, sir?

PITT
It is a fine example, sir, indeed,—
With that transparency amid the shades,
And those thin blue-green-grayish leafages
Behind the pillar in the background there,
Which seem the leaves themselves.—Ah, this is Quin.

[Moving to another picture.]

WILTSHIRE
Yes, Quin. A man of varied parts, though rough
And choleric at times. Yet, at his best,
As Falstaff, never matched, they say. But I
Had not the fate to see him in the flesh.

PITT
Churchill well carves him in his "Character":—
"His eyes, in gloomy socket taught to roll,
Proclaimed the sullen habit of his soul.
In fancied scenes, as in Life's real plan,
He could not for a moment sink the man:
Nature, in spite of all his skill, crept in;
Horatio, Dorax, Falstaff—stile 'twas Quin."
—He was at Bath when Gainsborough settled there
In that house in the Circus which we know.—
I like the portrait much.—The brilliancy
Of Gainsborough lies in this his double sway:
Sovereign of landscape he; of portraiture
Joint monarch with Sir Joshua.... Ah?—that's—hark!
Is that the patter of horses's hoofs
Along the road?

WILTSHIRE
I notice nothing, sir.

PITT
It is a gallop, growing quite distinct.
And—can it be a messenger for me!

WILTSHIRE
I hope no ugly European news
To stop the honour of this visit, sir!

[They listen. The gallop of the horse grows louder, and is checked at the door of the house. There is a hasty knocking, and a courier, splashed with mud from hard riding, is shown into the gallery. He presents a dispatch to PITT, who sits down and hurriedly opens it.]

PITT [to himself]
O heavy news indeed!... Disastrous; dire!

[He appears overcome as he sits, and covers his forehead with his hand.]

WILTSHIRE
I trust you are not ill, sir?

PITT [after some moments]
Could I have
A little brandy, sir, quick brought to me?

WILTSHIRE
In one brief minute.

[Brandy is brought in, and PITT takes it.]

PITT
Now leave me, please, alone. I'll call anon.
Is there a map of Europe handy here?

[WILTSHIRE fetches a map from the library, and spreads it before the minister. WILTSHIRE, courier, and servant go out.]

O God that I should live to see this day!

[He remains awhile in a profound reverie; then resumes the reading of the dispatch.]

"Defeated—the Allies—quite overthrown
At Austerlitz—last week."—Where's Austerlitz?
—But what avails it where the place is now;
What corpse is curious on the longitude
And situation of his cemetery!...
The Austrians and the Russians overcome,
That vast adventuring army is set free
To bend unhindered strength against our strand....
So do my plans through all these plodding years
Announce them built in vain!
His heel on Europe, monarchies in chains
To France, I am as though I had never been!

[He gloomily ponders the dispatch and the map some minutes longer. At last he rises with difficulty, and rings the bell. A servant enters.]

Call up my carriage, please you, now at once;
And tell your master I return to Bath
This moment—I may want a little help
In getting to the door here.

SERVANT
Sir, I will,
And summon you my master instantly.

[He goes out and re-enters with WILTSHIRE. PITT is assisted from the room.]

PITT
Roll up that map. 'Twill not be needed now
These ten years! Realms, laws, peoples, dynasties,
Are churning to a pulp within the maw
Of empire-making Lust and personal Gain!

[Exeunt PITT, WILTSHIRE, and the servant; and in a few minutes the carriage is heard driving off, and the
scene closes.]

SCENE VII

PARIS. A STREET LEADING TO THE TUILERIES

[It is night, and the dim oil lamps reveal a vast concourse of citizens of both sexes around the Palace
gates and in the neighbouring thoroughfares.]

SPIRIT OF THE YEARS [to the Spirit of Rumour]
Thou may'st descend and join this crowd awhile,
And speak what things shall come into they mouth.

SPIRIT SINISTER
I'll harken! I wouldn't miss it for the groans on another
Austerlitz!

[The Spirit of Rumour enters on the scene in the disguise of a young foreigner.]

SPIRIT [to a street-woman]
Lady, a late hour this to be afoot!

WOMAN
Poor profit, then, to me from my true trade,
Wherein hot competition is so rife
Already, since these victories brought to town
So many foreign jobbers in my line,
That I'd best hold my tongue from praise of fame!
However, one is caught by popular zeal,
And though five midnights have not brought a sou,
I, too, chant Jubilate like the rest. —

In courtesies have haughty monarchs vied
Towards the Conqueror! who, with men-at-arms
One quarter theirs, has vanquished by his nerve
Vast mustering four-hundred-thousand strong,
And given new tactics to the art of war
Unparalleled in Europe's history!

SPIRIT
What man is this, whose might thou blazonest so—
Who makes the earth to tremble, shakes old thrones,
And turns the plains to wilderness?

WOMAN
Dost ask
As ignorant, yet asking can define?
What mean you, traveller?

SPIRIT
I am a stranger here,
A wandering wight, whose life has not been spent
This side the globe, though I can speak the tongue.

WOMAN
Your air has truth in't; but your state is strange!
Had I a husband he should tackle thee.

SPIRIT
Dozens thou hast had—batches more than she
Samaria knew, if now thou hast not one!

WOMAN
Wilt take the situation from this hour?

SPIRIT
Thou know'st not what thy frailty asks, good dame!

WOMAN
Well, learn in small the Emperor's chronicle,
As gleaned from what my soldier-husbands say:—
some five-and-forty standards of his foes
Are brought to Paris, borne triumphantly
In proud procession through the surging streets,
Ever as brands of fame to shine aloft
In dim-lit senate-halls and city aisles.

SPIRIT
Fair Munich sparkled with festivity
As there awhile he tarried, and was met
By the gay Josephine your Empress here.—
There, too, Eugene—

WOMAN
Napoleon's stepson he—

SPIRIT

Received for gift the hand of fair Princess
Augusta [daughter of Bavaria's crown,
Forced from her plighted troth to Baden's heir],
And, to complete his honouring, was hailed
Successor to the throne of Italy.

WOMAN
How know you, ere this news has got abroad?

SPIRIT
Channels have I the common people lack.—
There, on the nonce, the forenamed Baden prince
Was joined to Stephanie Beauharnais, her
Who stands as daughter to the man we wait,
Some say as more.

WOMAN
They do? Then such not I.
Can revolution's dregs so soil thy soul
That thou shouldst doubt the eldest son thereof?
'Tis dangerous to insinuate nowadays!

SPIRIT
Right! Lady many-spoused, more charity
Upbrims in thee than in some loftier ones
Who would not name thee with their white-washed tongues.—
Enough. I am one whom, didst thou know my name,
Thou would'st not grudge a claim to speak his mind.

WOMAN
A thousand pardons, sir.

SPIRIT
Resume thy tale
If so thou wishest.

WOMAN
Nay, but you know best—-

SPIRIT
How laurelled progress through applauding crowds
Have marked his journey home. How Strasburg town,
Stuttgart, Carlsruhe, acclaimed him like the rest:
How pageantry would here have welcomed him,
Had not his speed outstript intelligence
—Now will a glimpse of him repay thee. Hark!

[Shouts arise and increase in the distance, announcing BONAPARTE'S approach.]

Well, Buonaparte has revived by land,
But not by sea. On that thwart element
Never will he incorporate his dream,
And float as master!

WOMAN
What shall hinder him?

SPIRIT
That which has hereto. England, so to say.

WOMAN
But she's in straits. She lost her Nelson now,
[A worthy man: he loved a woman well!]
George drools and babbles in a darkened room;
Her heaven-born Minister declines apace;
All smooths the Emperor's sway.

SPIRIT
Tales have two sides,
Sweet lady. Vamped-up versions reach thee here.—
That Austerlitz was lustrous none ignores,
But would it shock thy garrulousness to know
That the true measure of this Trafalgar—
Utter defeat, ay, France's naval death—
Your Emperor bade be hid?

WOMAN
The seer's gift
Has never plenteously endowed me, sir,
As in appearance you. But to plain sense
Thing's seem as stated.

SPIRIT
We'll let seemings be.—
But know, these English take to liquid life
Right patly—nursed therefor in infancy
By rimes and rains which creep into their blood,
Till like seeks like. The sea is their dry land,
And, as on cobbles you, they wayfare there.

WOMAN
Heaven prosper, then, their watery wayfarings
If they'll leave us the land!—

[The Imperial carriage appears.]

The Emperor!—
Long live the Emperor!—He's the best by land.

[BONAPARTE'S carriage arrives, without an escort. The street lamps shine in, and reveal the EMPRESS JOSEPHINE seated beside him. The plaudits of the people grow boisterous as they hail him Victor of Austerlitz. The more active run after the carriage, which turns in from the Rue St. Honore to the Carrousel, and thence vanishes into the Court of the Tuileries.]

WOMAN
May all success attend his next exploit!

SPIRIT
Namely: to put the knife in England's trade,
And teach her treaty-manners—if he can!

WOMAN
I like not your queer knowledge, creepy man.
There's weirdness in your air. I'd call you ghost
Had not the Goddess Reason laid all such
Past Mother Church's cunning to restore.
—Adieu. I'll not be yours to-night. I'd starve first!

[She withdraws. The crowd wastes away, and the Spirit vanishes.]

SCENE VIII

PUTNEY. BOWLING GREEN HOUSE

[PITT'S bedchamber, from the landing without. It is afternoon. At the back of the room as seen through the doorway is a curtained bed, beside which a woman sits, the LADY HESTER STANHOPE. Bending over a table at the front of the room is SIR WALTER FARQUHAR, the physician. PARSLOW the footman and another servant are near the door. TOMLINE, the Bishop of Lincoln, enters.]

FARQUHAR [in a subdued voice]
I grieve to call your lordship up again,
But symptoms lately have disclosed themselves
That mean the knell to the frail life in him.
And whatsoever thing of gravity
It may be needful to communicate,
Let them be spoken now. Time may not serve
If they be much delayed.

TOMLINE
Ah, stands it this?...
The name of his disease is—Austerlitz!
His brow's inscription has been Austerlitz

From that dire morning in the month just past
When tongues of rumour twanged the word across
From its hid nook on the Moravian plains.

FARQUHAR
And yet he might have borne it, had the weight
Of governmental shackles been unclasped,
Even partly, from his limbs last Lammastide,
When that despairing journey to the King
At Gloucester Lodge by Wessex shore was made
To beg such. But relief the King refused.
"Why want you Fox? What—Grenville and his friends?"
He harped. "You are sufficient without these—
Rather than Fox, why, give me civil war!"
And fibre that would rather snap than shrink
Held out no longer. Now the upshot nears.

[LADY HESTER STANHOPE turns her head and comes forward.]

LADY HESTER
I am grateful you are here again, good friend!
He's sleeping some light seconds; but once more
Has asked for tidings of Lord Harrowby,
And murmured of his mission to Berlin
As Europe's haggard hope; if, sure, it be
That any hope remain!

TOMLINE
There's no news yet.—
These several days while I have been sitting by him
He has inquired the quarter of the wind,
And where that moment beaked the stable-cock.
When I said "East," he answered "That is well!
Those are the breezes that will speed him home!"
So cling his heart-strings to his country's cause.

FARQUHAR
I fear that Wellesley's visit here by now
Strung him to tensest strain. He quite broke down,
And has fast faded since.

LADY HESTER
Ah! now he wakes.
Please come and speak to him as you would wish [to TOMLINE].

[LADY HESTER, TOMLINE,and FARQUHAR retire behind the bed, where in a short time voices are heard
in prayer. Afterwards the Bishop goes to a writing-table, and LADY HESTER comes to the doorway.

Steps are heard on the stairs, and PITT'S friend ROSE, the President of the Board of Trade, appears on the landing and makes inquiries.]

LADY HESTER [whispering]
He wills the wardenry of his affairs
To his old friend the Bishop. But his words
Bespeak too much anxiety for me,
And underrate his services so far
That he has doubts if his high deeds deserve
Such size of recognition by the State
As would award slim pensions to his kin.
He had been fain to write down his intents,
But the quill dropped from his unmuscled hand.—
Now his friend Tomline pens what he dictates
And gleans the lippings of his last desires.

[ROSE and LADY HESTER turn. They see the Bishop bending over the bed with a sheet of paper on which he has previously been writing. A little later he dips a quill and holds it within the bed-curtain, spreading the paper beneath. A thin white hand emerges from behind the curtain and signs the paper. The Bishop beckons forward the two servants, who also sign.

FARQUHAR on one side of the bed, and TOMLINE on the other, are spoken to by the dying man. The Bishop afterwards withdraws from the bed and comes to the landing where the others are.]

TOMLINE
A list of his directions has been drawn,
And feeling somewhat more at mental ease
He asks Sir Walter if he has long to live.
Farquhar just answered, in a soothing tone,
That hope still frailly breathed recovery.
At this my dear friend smiled and shook his head,
As if to say: "I can translate your words,
But I reproach not friendship's lullabies."

ROSE
Rest he required; and rest was not for him.

[FARQUHAR comes forward as they wait.]

FARQUHAR
His spell of concentration on these things,
Determined now, that long have wasted him,
Have left him in a numbing lethargy,
From which I fear he may not rouse to strength
For speech with earth again.

ROSE
But hark. He does.

[The listen.]

PITT
My country! How I leave my country!...

TOMLINE
Ah,—
Immense the matter those poor words contain!

ROSE
Still does his soul stay wrestling with that theme,
And still it will, even semi-consciously,
Until the drama's done.

[They continue to converse by the doorway in whispers. PITT sinks slowly into a stupor, from which he never awakens.]

SPIRIT OF THE PITIES [to Spirit of the Years]
Do you intend to speak to him ere the close?

SPIRIT OF THE YEARS
Nay, I have spoke too often! Time and time,
When all Earth's light has lain on the nether side,
And yapping midnight winds have leapt on the roofs,
And raised for him an evil harlequinade
Of national disasters in long train,
That tortured him with harrowing grimace,
Now I would leave him to pass out in peace,
And seek the silence unperturbedly.

SPIRIT SINISTER
Even ITS official Spirit can show ruth
At man's fag end, when his destruction's sure!

SPIRIT OF THE YEARS
It suits us ill to cavil each with each.
I might retort. I only say to thee
ITS slaves we are: ITS slaves must ever be!

CHORUS [aerial music]
Yea, from the Void we fetch, like these,
And tarry till That please
To null us by Whose stress we emanate.—
Our incorporeal sense,
Our overseeings, our supernal state,
Our readings Why and Whence,
Are but the flower of Man's intelligence;

And that but an unreckoned incident
Of the all-urging Will, raptly magnipotent.

[A gauze of shadow overdraws.]

FOOTNOTES

(1) - Schlegel.

(2) - Introduction to the Choephori.

(3) - It is now called an Epic-drama, Footnote 1909.

(4) - Through this tangle of intentions the writer has in the main followed Thiers, whose access to documents would seem to authenticate his details of the famous scheme for England's ruin.

(5) - These historic facings, which, I believe, won for the local [Footnote old 39th: regiment the nickname of "Green Linnets," have been changed for no apparent reason. Footnote They are now restored—1909

(6) - The remains of the lonely hut occupied by the beacon-keepers, consisting of some half-buried brickbats, and a little mound of peat overgrown with moss, are still visible on the elevated spot referred to. The two keepers themselves, and their eccentricities and sayings are traditionary, with a slight disguise of names.

(7) - "Le projet existe encore aux archives de la marine que Napoleon consultait incessamment; il sentait que cette marine depuis Louis XIV. avait fait de grandes choses: le plan de l'Expedition d'Egypte et de la descente en Angleterre se trouvaient au ministere de la marine."—CAPEFIGUE: L'Europe pendant le Consulat et l'Empire.

(8) - This weather-beaten old building, though now an hotel, is but little altered.

(9) - Soph. Trach. 1266-72.

(10) - This scene is a little antedated, to include it in the Act to which it essentially belongs.

(11) - "Quel bonhour que je n'aie aucun enfant pour recueillir mon horrible heritage et qui soit charge du poids de mon nom!"— [Footnote Extract from the poignant letter to his wife written on this night.— See Lanfrey iii. 374.

(12) - In those days the hind-part of the harbour adjoining this scene was so named, and at high tides the waves washed across the isthmus at a point called "The Narrows."

(13) - This General's name should, it is said, be pronounced in three syllables, nearly PRESH-EV-SKY.

Thomas Hardy OM was an English novelist, whose Victorian realism was inspired by the Romantic movement, particularly Wordsworth, and by Dickens, who was also critical of much of Victorian society. Unlike Dickens, though, who writes primarily about cities and towns, Hardy sets much of his work in the semi-fictional country of Wessex, focusing on the decline of rural practice in England. He was known first for his novels, but towards the end of his life his poetry began to see publication and he is now considered one of the major poets of English literature, influencing various poets in the 1950-60s, most notably Philip Larkin.

Hardy was born in the hamlet of Upper Bockhampton in the Stinsford parish about three miles east of Dorchester in Dorset, England, on 2nd June 1840, in a two-storey brick and thatch cottage. His father Thomas worked as a self-employed master mason and local builder contractor, while also playing the violin. His mother, Jemima, a former maid-servant and cook, was well-read in Latin and French romances in English translation, and she enjoyed retelling the folk stories and legends of the region while she educated her son until the age of eight when he first attended the local National School in Lower Bockhampton, which had opened that year in 1848. The school was run by the National Society for Promoting the Education of the Poor in the Principles of the Established Church. From his parents, he received all of the interests and passions which would shape his writing and his life; the interest in architecture and love of music from his father, and his interest in rural lifestyles and traditions from his mother, along with a passion for literature. The Hardy family were descended from the Le Hardy family, who had resided on the Isle of Jersey since the 15th century. They had several ancestors of significant import, though at the turn of the eighteenth century the family had experienced a sharp economic collapse, a circumstance which would become key to the narrative of Tess of the d'Urbervilles. Maul Turner writes of Hardy's childhood that "apart from parental influences, Hardy's childhood was dominated by two things: the local church, and the natural world around him".

After two years at the National School, his mother enrolled him at a non-conformist school in Dorchester, run by the British and Foreign School Society, and while there he learnt Latin and French, amongst other subjects. To compliment his education, he read Greek and Roman classics in translation, and the Bible, which he knew in close detail, and he expressed a fondness for romances. In addition to his favourite authors, William Harrison Ainsworth, Walter Scott and Alexandre Dumas, he read Shakespeare's tragedies and, although ultimately he rather enjoyed school, he preferred to read books in relative solitude. While he was in Dorset, he bore witness to the decline of the traditions of the pastoral society in the face of the rise of industrialism.

Deemed unlikely by his parents and his teachers to lead a successful scholarly or clerical career, Hardy gained an apprenticeship in 1856 at the age of sixteen to John Hicks, a local architect whose speciality was in church restoration. The occupation saw him travelling extensively around Dorset, while back at the office he met another apprentice, Henry Bastow, with a similar interest in classical literature, poetry and religious matters. His only opportunity to read was in the morning before work between the hours of five and eight, and while he was working and reading here he met the poet William Barnes, also a local schoolmaster, who published poetry focusing on rural life in local dialects, and it is quite possible that it was this encounter which encouraged him to write poetry about similar themes. Within this poetry are various ideas which he picked up while on his apprenticeship, and he showed his poetry to Horace Moule, son of the vicar and a student at Queen's College, Cambridge, who, eight years Hardy's senior, became his best friend and mentor and encouraged him in his reading of Greek tragedy and more contemporary English literature. The most significant works of literature published at this time, which will no doubt have influenced Hardy, were Alfred Tennyson's poems Idylls of the King, George Meredith's Richard Feverel and Evan Harrington, Wilkie Collins's The Woman in White and George Eliot's The Mill on the Floss. Alongside these works of fiction was Charles Darwin's The Origin of Species, which had a profound influence on Hardy.

Suspending his architectural apprenticeship and heading for London in April 1862, he rented lodgings at 3, Clarence Place at Kilburn, near the Edgware Road. This move is widely considered to be the result of an unsuccessful love affair; he had already had infatuations with two girls in Dorset, who "scorned him as too young", and just prior to his move he had proposed to and been rejected by a Dorchester girl, Mary Waight, also significantly his senior. These rejections arguably encouraged him to move and begin afresh in new surroundings. While in London, he spent five years working as Arthur Blomfield's assistant architect, a noted restorer and designer of churches. Blomfield valued Hardy's work for him and put his name forward to be a member of the Architectural Association.

Meanwhile, he attended Charles Dickens's public lecture and spent time exploring the scientific and cultural offerings of London society, visiting museums and galleries, and seeing plays and operas. Further reading included the word of Herbert Spencer, Thomas Henry Huxley, John Stuart Mill, John Ruskin and Charles Darwin. The combined effect of these writers was to cause him to abandon plans of ordination in the Anglican Church, becoming increasingly disillusioned with the more institutional forms of Christianity. His own poetry flourished, spurred on by reading Robert Browning and Algernon Charles Swinburne, though it was still rejected for publication. He wrote the satire How I Built Myself a House in 1865, published in Chambers Journal and which was the first of his work to achieve recognition, winning him a prize. He also persevered with his poetry, though it remained unpublished.

By 1867 Hardy had grown tired of London and returned to Bockhampton to resume his work with John Hicks. He embarked on a love affair with his cousin, Tryphena, who lived nearby and, though there is little historical evidence of their relationship, had a profound effect on his writing at the time and appears in various guises throughout the poetry he wrote then, while also in the more obviously dedicated poem 'Thoughts of Phena'. He now began his first novel, The Poor Man and the Lady, which he submitted to Alexander Macmillan, a publishing house. Though Macmillan himself chose not to publish it, he encouraged Hardy to continue writing, and Hardy was advised to concentrate on his plotting. John Hicks's death in 1869 caused Hardy to move to Weymouth seeking employment, and at the same time he began Desperate Remedies, also refused by Macmillan but later published anonymously in three volumes by William Tinsley, in 1871. This publication saw him resolve to dedicate himself fully to his writing, though he was not yet in a position to achieve financial security or literary success. His second published novel, Under the Greenwood Tree, appeared in 1872 and its favourable reception encouraged the publication of A Pair of Blue Eyes in 1873, the most autobiographical of his novels. Next came Far From the Madding Crowd in 1874, bringing with it critical acclaim, the attention of the public and ultimately financial success. 1878 saw more success with The Return of the Native, and the ensuing years saw him rise to ever greater popularity. By now he had developed the fictional Wessex and resolved to set all of his novels there.

It was while he was working on the restoration of a church in St. Juliot, Cornwall, that he met Emma Lavinia Gifford, the local rector's sister-in-law. Captivated by her looks and her admiration for him, he fell in love with her and she would encourage his prose and poetry writing, attracted by his literary capabilities. It took them four years to marry, though, on 17th September 1874 in St Peters Church, Paddington, London. They were both thirty at marriage, though he thought she looked younger and she thought he looked older. None of Hardy's family attended the service. In 1885 the couple settled near Dorchester at Max Gate, a large mid-Victorian villa, designed by Hardy and where he spent the rest of his life. He felt very comfortable there, calling it his country retreat. The Mayor of Casterbridge was published in 1886, and its fictional setting bears many similarities to Dorchester, the market town which he knew so well. He and Emma journeyed to Italy in 1887, returning via Paris and London.

Tess of the d'Urbervilles was published in 1891 to the shock of the prudish Victorian audience who were dismayed by with the cruel presentation of a young girl's seduction and ruination by a rakish aristocrat. It only saw publication after Hardy made extensive alterations to its plot, editing or deleting vast passages. His last novel, Jude the Obscure, suffered the same levels of public outcry when it was published in 1895, and the uproar over these two novels so disturbed him that he returned to poetry, regarded by him and his audience as a purer form of artistic expression. He had not been able to make enough money as a young man to live off his poetry, but now as an adult living off the success of his novels he was able to survive comfortably, and even had a collection of his earlier poems published under the title Wessex Poems, in 1898. Meanwhile, in 1896 Emma had introduced him to the fashionable new pastime of cycling and he bought a high-quality Rover Cobb bicycle, frequently touring the Dorset countryside with his wife. They travelled extensively, to Paris, the Continent and throughout England, along with a visit to Belgium.

Hardy spent the years between 1903 and 1908 writing The Dynasts, and epic poem in blank verse about the Napoleonic Wars, and his literary authority saw him honoured by the University of Aberdeen with an honourary degree in 1905, bringing with it recognition as one of the most outstanding British authors. George V conferred on him the Order of Merit in 1910 and he was awarded the gold medal of the Royal Society of Literature in 1912. Further to his honourary degree at Aberdeen, Cambridge University named him a Doctor of Letters, his popularity continuing to grow the entire time. WIth this popularity came the dramatisation and performance of various works, and in 1914 the adaptation of The Dynasts was performed at Kingsway Theatre in London. He now proceeded to sell or donate the majority of his manuscripts, either to museums or collectors.

Emma died suddenly on 27th November 1912, and despite having grown increasingly estranged he was greatly affected by her passing, reproaching himself after her burial for not having realised the extent of her illness. He proceeded to write numerous poems expressing nostalgia for their happier times in youth, and after her death he was now taken care of by his niece and a young woman, Florence Dagdale. She was shy and charming with literary aspirations of her own, having published a few books for children, and again her admiration for him led to his infatuation with her. They married on 6th February 1914, though the wedding quickly deteriorated with it became apparent that Hardy preferred "spending much of each day closeted in his study". By now, he was in his seventies, though in spite of his ages he campaigned in favour of British involvement in the First World War. Many great writers visited him at Max Gate, for he left less and less.

In 1924 hew witnessed a stage production of Tess of the d'Urbervilles, a performance so powerful that Hardy promptly became infatuated with the young actress playing Tess. From 1920 to 1927 he worked, in secret, on his autobiography, which was published in two volumes in 1928 and 1930 as the work of Florence Hardy. She made various emendations to the text, having typed the manuscripts, probably reducing the references to Emma and adding anecdotes and referring to letters. His 87th birthday passed, and he seemed increasingly weaker, staying in bed for long periods, until in 1927 he fell gravely ill, dying on the 11th January 1928. Just prior to his death, he asked Florence to read a verse from The Rubaiyat of Omar Khayyam,

Oh, Thou, who Man of baser Earth didst make,
And ev'n with Paradise devise the snake:
For all the Sin wherewith the Face of Man
Is blackened - Man's forgiveness give - and take!

His body was cremated and the ashes interred in Poet's Corner in the South Transept in Westminster Abbey. The official of the two funerals was attended by the then Prime Minister Stanley Baldwin, leader of the Opposition Ramsay MacDonald, the heads of Oxford and Cambridge University colleges where Hardy had been honoured, and various significant literary figures such as James Barrie, George Bernard Shaw and Rudyard Kipling. Meanwhile, his heart was buried alongside his first wife in Stinsford churchyard, Dorchester. He is best remembered by Evelyn Hardy, the critic, who writes "Hardy's life was not primarily one of action. He was by nature a scholar and a writer: it is what goes on in the mind that holds us, and Hardy's was rich with stored impressions".

THOMAS HARDY – A CONCISE BIBLIOGRAPHY

Prose

Hardy divided his novels and collected short stories into three types

Novels of Character and Environment
The Poor Man and the Lady (1867, unpublished and now lost)
Under the Greenwood Tree: A Rural Painting of the Dutch School (1872)
Far from the Madding Crowd (1874)
The Return of the Native (1878)
The Mayor of Casterbridge: The Life and Death of a Man of Character (1886)
The Woodlanders (1887)

Wessex Tales (1888, a collection of short stories)
Tess of the d'Urbervilles: A Pure Woman Faithfully Presented (1891)
Life's Little Ironies (1894, a collection of short stories)
Jude the Obscure (1895)

Romances and Fantasies
A Pair of Blue Eyes: A Novel (1873)
The Trumpet-Major (1880)
Two on a Tower: A Romance (1882)
A Group of Noble Dames (1891, a collection of short stories)
The Well-Beloved: A Sketch of a Temperament (1897) (first published as a serial from 1892)

Novels of Ingenuity
Desperate Remedies: A Novel (1871)
The Hand of Ethelberta: A Comedy in Chapters (1876)
A Laodicean: A Story of To-day (1881)

Short Stories
How I Built Myself A House (1865)
Destiny and a Blue Cloak (1874)
The Thieves Who Couldn't Stop Sneezing (1877)
The Duchess of Hamptonshire (1878)
The Distracted Preacher (1879)
Fellow-Townsmen (1880)
The Honourable Laura (1881)
What The Shepherd Saw (1881)
A Tradition of Eighteen Hundred and Four (1882)
The Three Strangers (1883)
The Romantic Adventures of a Milkmaid (1883)
Interlopers at the Knap (1884)
A Mere Interlude (1885)
A Tryst at an Ancient Earthwork (1885)
Alicia's Diary (1887)
The Waiting Supper (1887–88)
The Withered Arm (1888)
A Tragedy of Two Ambitions (1888)
The First Countess of Wessex (1889)
Anna, Lady Baxby (1890)
The Lady Icenway (1890)
Lady Mottisfont (1890)
The Lady Penelope (1890)
The Marchioness of Stonehenge (1890)

Squire Petrick's Lady (1890)
Barbara of the House of Grebe (1890)
The Melancholy Hussar of The German Legion (1890)
Absent-Mindedness in a Parish Choir (1891)
The Winters and the Palmleys (1891)
For Conscience' Sake (1891)
Incident in Mr. Crookhill's Life (1891)
The Doctor's Legend (1891)
Andrey Satchel and the Parson and Clerk (1891)
The History of the Hardcomes (1891)
Netty Sargent's Copyhold (1891)
On The Western Circuit (1891)
A Few Crusted Characters: Introduction (1891)
The Superstitious Man's Story (1891)
Tony Kytes, the Arch-Deceiver (1891)
To Please His Wife (1891)
The Son's Veto (1891)
Old Andrey's Experience as a Musician (1891)
Our Exploits At West Poley (1892–93)
Master John Horseleigh, Knight (1893)
The Fiddler of the Reels (1893)
An Imaginative Woman (1894)
The Spectre of the Real (1894)
A Committee-Man of 'The Terror' (1896)
The Duke's Reappearance (1896)
The Grave by the Handpost (1897)
A Changed Man (1900)
Enter a Dragoon (1900)
Blue Jimmy: The Horse Stealer (1911)
Old Mrs. Chundle (1929)
The Unconquerable (1992)

Poetry Collections
Wessex Poems and Other Verses (1898)
Poems of the Past and the Present (1901)
Time's Laughingstocks and Other Verses (1909)
Satires of Circumstance (1914)
Moments of Vision (1917)
Collected Poems (1919)
Late Lyrics and Earlier with Many Other Verses (1923)
Human Shows, Far Phantasies, Songs and Trifles (1925)
Winter Words in Various Moods and Metres (1928)

Drama

The Dynasts: An Epic-Drama of the War with Napoleon (verse drama)

The Dynasts, Part 1 (1904)

The Dynasts, Part 2 (1906)

The Dynasts, Part 3 (1908)

The Famous Tragedy of the Queen of Cornwall at Tintagel in Lyonnesse (1923) (one-act play)